35
dumb
THINGS
WELL-INTENDED
PEOPLE
SAY

SURPRISING THINGS WE SAY
THAT WIDEN THE DIVERSITY GAP

DR. MAURA CULLEN

EXPERTS
ACADEMY
PRESS

An Imprint of Morgan James Publishing

35 dumb THINGS WELL-INTENDED PEOPLE SAY

ISBN: 978-1-60037-491-3 (Paperback)

Published by:

MORGAN · JAMES™
THE ENTREPRENEURIAL PUBLISHER™
www.morganjamespublishing.com

Morgan James Publishing, LLC
1225 Franklin Ave Suite 325
Garden City, NY 11530-1693
Toll Free 800-485-4943
www.MorganJamesPublishing.com

Cover Design by:
(c) 2008 by Clarence Jessop

Interior Design by:
Rachel Lopez
rachel@r2cdesign.com

Habitat
for Humanity®
Peninsula
Building Partner

Disclaimer

This book is designed to provide information on how to best handle issues of diversity. It is sold with the understanding that the publisher and author are not engaged in rendering legal, accounting or otherwise professional services. If legal or other expert assistance is required, the services of a competent professional should be sought.

Every effort has been made to make this book as complete and accurate as possible. However, there may be mistakes, both typographical and in content. Therefore, this text should be used only as a general guide and not as the ultimate source of handling sensitive issues such as diversity. Furthermore, this book contains information solely gleaned from the author's own experiences and background.

The purpose of this book is to educate and entertain. The author and publisher shall have neither liability nor responsibility to any person or entity with respect to any loss or damage caused, or alleged to have been caused, directly or indirectly, by the information contained in this book.

Dedication

To my parents, Maureen and Tom Cullen who lovingly showed us what is most important in life—family.

To the love of my life, Dawn, even though I doubted myself at times you never wavered. Thank you.

Praise for *35 Dumb Things Well-Intended People Say*

"Our success and future prosperity as a people and a nation is dependent on our understanding and responding to each other with wisdom and compassion. This book shows you how."

- BRIAN TRACY, *author of* The Psychology of Achievement and Goals!

"Good intentions are not enough as Dr. Maura Cullen so skillfully points out in her book. This well written, down to earth, no blame, insightful book is a resource every one interested in developing authentic relationships across difference must have. If you ever found yourself unsure of what to say to someone different from you (and said nothing) then this book will provide you valuable tools to be more effective every day."

- JUDITH H. KATZ, ED. D., *Executive Vice President, The Kaleel Jamison Consulting Group. Inc., author of* White Awareness: Handbook for Anti-Racism Training Inclusion, Breakthrough: Unleashing the Real Power of Diversity *and* Be BIG; Step Up, Step Out, Be Bold

"Dr. Cullen is clearly the go-to expert on diversity. I was personally astounded by how many 'dumb' things I say and how my honestly well-intended statements could potentially hurt my relationships, and credibility, with others. This is a must-read book for every student and executive in America who wants to understand what it takes to respect and work with today's diverse global workforce."

- BRENDON BURCHARD, *author of* The Student Leadership Guide *and* Life's Golden Ticket

"This is the book that explains why people get offended by many of our everyday comments and shows us practical steps to improve our effectiveness around issues of diversity. Good for students as well as faculty and staff."

- DARYL G. SMITH, *Professor of Education and Psychology, Claremont Graduate University*

"35 Dumb Things Well-Intended People Say provides extraordinary insight into one of the most important issues of our times, diversity. Maura's no non-sense approach stimulates conversation not stifles it."

- RICHARD RAMOS, *Latino Coalition for Faith & Community Leadership*

"35 Dumb Things is phenomenal in tackling diversity issues in an honest, humorous and straightforward manner. Not to read this book would be Dumb Thing #36!"

- DR. ANDREA *Kandel, Executive Director, National Conference for Community & Justice*

Praise for Maura

"Over my twenty plus years working in nonprofits, I have taken part in many diversity training sessions and found Maura Cullen's workshop to be the best. Maura uses humor and real life situations to which we can all relate."

- SUSAN B. *Dunn, President and CEO, United Way of the Capital Area, Hartford, CT*

"Having been involved in diversity efforts in the legal profession for many years, I know that "diversity" is a complicated and divisive issue, often rooted in emotions deep within us. Dr. Cullen has an uncanny ability to bring those emotions to the surface and challenge her participants to think about the issues in ways never thought of before. I highly recommend her creative and engaging approach to perhaps the most significant workplace issue of our time."

> - ASKER A. *Saeed, Esq.*
>
> *President, South Asian Bar Association of Connecticut*

"Maura Cullen does not merely train participants. She engages, motivates, and challenges them to set aside ingrained preconceptions they may have about those who are different from themselves. They come away with more than the typical training handouts. They come away with a visual and visceral experience that helps them to better understand others' perspectives."

> - SHARON MANGIERI, *Director of Employee Relations*
>
> *& Training, Office of Human Resources Western*
>
> *New England College, MA*

"Maura Cullen has demonstrated that she is truly a leader among the finest trainers / consultants on the international campus circuit today. She relates to and communicates with students so effectively, her humor and charisma hold their media-soaked attention... even those disillusioned by and with political correctness."

> - JANICE ROBINSON
>
> *University of British Columbia, Canada*

"I am a returning RA and dreaded coming to diversity training. Maura kept us engaged for an incredible five hours through her activities, stories and humor. She made diversity easy to understand without making anyone feel guilty or angry and related it to our resident assistant role. By far this is the most enjoyable diversity training I have EVER attended!"

- ANDY WEINKAUF

University of Wisconsin-Platteville, WI

"In the short time that Dr. Cullen was with us, she forever changed our organization for the better. The training really helped people see the positive aspects of our work environment and also empowered staff to take active, constructive roles for positive change within our organization. To be sure, we will be asking Dr. Cullen to return in the future!"

- DR. SUSAN M. HANSEN

San Jose State University, CA

"I have been doing diversity work for over 20 years. There is no one that I respect more, or would recommend more highly as a trainer, facilitator or speaker than Maura Cullen. Her style, skills and knowledge make her one of the best in the business."

- REV. DR. JAMIE WASHINGTON, *President,*

The Washington Consulting Group

"Maura's work is professional, engaging, genuine and sincere, but most of all it is framed with integrity, warmth, reality and appropriate humor. If you want a sensational educational outcome for your program or special event ...Maura is more."

- DAVID A. HOLMES, *La Trobe University, Australia*

Acknowledgements

There are a number of people who I need to acknowledge, for without their support and guidance, this book would never have been written.

Marlene Oulton, my editor and friend, thanks for keeping me laughing and on track with your insightful guidance.

Also a big thank you to all of you who helped along this journey: Jeanine Bessette, Staci Buchwald, Brendon Burchard, Paulette Dalpes, Nancy Hunter-Denney, Francesca Verri Gove, Susan Hansen, Jill Hoppenjans, Andrea Kandel, Samuel Lurie, James Malinchak, Jackie Simpson, Daryl Smith, Kathy Sisneros, Dawn Teagarden, Jamie Washington and Marvin Worthy. Your support and suggestions were significant.

A Note From Maura

Have you ever been afraid of saying the wrong thing and so said nothing at all? Or perhaps something came out of your mouth that you wish you could take back immediately? That's how I was, and at times continue to be, especially as it relates to issues of diversity and inclusion. There I was, a very well-intended person who would never intentionally cause harm to someone else, yet I was clueless to the impact I was having on those around me. I would make statements like, "Some of my best friends are..." or "I don't think of you as..." and not understand why some people would be offended.

Over time I realized that there were a slew of common statements and questions which people would say and that would unintentionally cause harm or offend people. In *35 Dumb Things Well-Intended People Say*, I provide an abbreviated list of everyday comments made by everyday people. I should confess here that I didn't have to do much research for this book as I am guilty of having said many of these. Everyday, I witness kind and well-intentioned people saying over and over many of the Dumb Things listed in the book.

35 Dumb Things Well-Intended People Say offers insight and information on how to transform many of the conversations we have around issues of diversity. With all of my heart, I believe that if people knew not only what, but also why some of the things they say are harmful, then they would stop saying them. I also wanted to condense as much practical information as possible into a short but powerful book so that everyday people would take this opportunity to enhance their lives as well as those around them. This book looks to simplify that which confuses us and offers suggestions to improve the quality of our interactions. I trust you will benefit from reading this as much as I did writing it.

Contents

SETTING THE STAGE
Chapter One

This book was written to inspire you to achieve more inclusive, compassionate and effective communication patterns.

It will demonstrate just how common it is for well-intended people to inadvertently cause harm without ever knowing they have done so. People often make statements which they intend to be supportive or complimentary, but end up being problematic. Meant as joining statements, these remarks often have the opposite effect and end up creating a larger divide, and at times inciting feelings of anger. Ultimately, the problem continues to repeat itself over and over because many of us are not aware that we have done or said anything offensive in the first place! Your relationships with colleagues and family members for example, may be compromised everyday, yet you may not be aware of the damage being done. This is definitely preventable, as you will see in the chapters which follow

This book offers you practical ways to quickly transform the quality and effectiveness of your interactions. You will learn how by making small adjustments to what you say can reap huge rewards in your personal and professional life. It will offer valuable insights as to how your everyday comments impact others.

Acquiring knowledge of these *35 Dumb Things* is a great start to improving your relationships, both personally and professionally. Having this knowledge is the first step, but learning the necessary skills to apply this knowledge is crucial. No matter how hard we try to avoid offensive or hurtful language, we will never be perfect. The true test of our consciousness happens after we mess up, and how well we respond to our mistakes and the action we take. This book breaks down these 3 very important steps: Knowledge, Skills and Action, and shows you how to implement strategies to prevent potential hurtful words and actions.

The first section of this book will provide the skill segment of the knowledge, skill and action equation. If you are like me, you may be tempted to skip the 10 Core Concepts and just read the *35 Dumb Things*. This would be a mistake. The 10 Core Concepts are equally, if not more, critical to understand than the actual dumb statements themselves.

The knowledge segment will consist of actual *35 Dumb Things Well- Intended People Say*, and the action segment will be found at the end in the section entitled, 6 Smart Steps For Well-Intended People.

How important is it to adopt all three of these steps? Let me share with you a real life example of when I put only two of the three steps into action. The end result speaks for itself.

Many years ago, I attended a wedding where all of the guests were white with the exception of one couple who were African American. My friends and I were standing in the bar area and I noticed that when the man of color went to get a drink, he was asked for identification by the white bartender. I found this interesting because he was the only person I noticed being asked to show identification. He was clearly older than me and my friends and yet none of us were challenged by the bartender. Believing this could possibly be an act of racism, I mentioned my observation to my friends. My friends encouraged me to just let it go and to take a day off from my "social justice mission." This I would not do. So for the next twenty minutes I observed the frequency of people being asked for identification. Not one other person was asked! What put me over the top and ignited my need to take action was when a boy of about fourteen ordered, and was given, two beers by this same bartender.

At that point I marched up to the bartender and pronounced him to be "a racist asshole!" Granted, this was not my finest moment. In retrospect, I wish I had approached the bartender in a more calm and informative manner, yet I was incensed at what

I had perceived to be his racist attitude. This is a clear example of what happens when good people want to take action to eradicate injustice yet not having the skills to be effective.

Was this an effective intervention? Did it seek to educate? Was it done in a respectful manner? The answer to all of those questions is no. In my eagerness to practice my new skills for confronting acts of intolerance I was disrespectful and ineffective. Like any new skill you won't be perfect in the beginning. Yet in order to improve your skills you need to start somewhere. Don't be afraid to make mistakes because the bigger mistake is to do nothing.

Keeping in mind the model of Knowledge, Skills, Action, I possessed the knowledge and took immediate action, but lacked the skills which resulted in a less than desirable outcome. Having a solid understanding of the 10 Core Concepts is essential towards building these critical skills.

WHAT THIS BOOK IS

This book shares lessons I have learned throughout my career as an experienced diversity trainer and speaker in the field of social justice. As I continue to grow and learn about issues of diversity and inclusion, I am certain that these conversations do not have to be combative or divisive. You will soon recognize this spirit in the pages which follow, as I offer you the best practices I have found in creating more inclusive organizations.

On the other hand, my intention is not to eliminate all of the adversity which often accompanies our conversations around diversity issues. In fact, I strongly believe that a certain amount of conflict and discomfort is essential to initiate change. However, I believe we can all do a better job at lessening the levels of incivility by increasing the levels of knowledge and respect.

WHAT THIS BOOK IS NOT

This book is not an in-depth look at the complexities of social justice and oppression. It doesn't offer theories, nor will it attempt to explain them. It is not meant to do anything except offer insight about the power and impact of everyday language.

Today, as we embrace a global economy, more and more individuals and organizations understand the benefits and necessity of leveraging the diversity of experience, cultures and perspectives within the workforce. On a personal level, families encounter this diversity, tensions arise and feelings are hurt because difference is not discussed in a practical way. As our national populations grows and diversifies, so does our level of discomfort in having dialogue around difference. As a result, many of our conversations have us walking on eggshells.

One of the cornerstones of being able to take the sting out of many conversations around diversity, or any topic for that matter, revolves around basic skills of being courteous and respectful of others. Yet common courtesy is not enough to shift the dynamics necessary to create a more inclusive community. Such change requires a strong base of knowledge and the understanding of core competencies and skills.

Over the years I have said and used many of the following "dumb" statements on more than one occasion. Most of the time, I was totally clueless as to the impact I was having on the other person. I try very hard not to intentionally cause harm to anyone, but just because I don't mean to cause harm doesn't mean that my actions or words still don't hurt or offend the other person. This is one of the core concepts, intent vs. impact. Just because we have good intentions does not mean that the other person is not negatively impacted. This concept will be further explained later.

POLITICAL CORRECTNESS

According to the American Heritage Dictionary, the term politically correct is defined as: "relating to or supporting broad social, political, and educational change, especially to redress historical injustices in matters such as race, class, gender, and sexual orientation." The furor over the concept of political correctness, also referred to as being "PC", has widened the divide on our conversations around issues of diversity. Often used with an accusatory and negative tone, political correctness is defined by various perspectives. For some, political correctness is an intrusion on their first amendment rights. This group of individuals believes that living in the United States guarantees our basic right to say what we want regardless of what others may think or feel. This freedom of speech is a core and fundamental right stated in the United States Constitution. Therefore, the creation of "hate speech codes" or other kinds of legislation which limits speech is seen as an assault on our First Amendment rights.

For others, political correctness looks to secure another fundamental right of The Constitution; the right to life, liberty and the pursuit of happiness. It is also reflected in the last line of the Pledge of Allegiance, "With liberty and justice for all." Non-discrimination laws and legislation allow people to be free from harassment and discrimination which may impede their right for equal opportunity.

Some limits already exist to our First Amendment rights, such as not being able to falsely shout "fire" in a public building, which was created with the intention of keeping people free from harm. Creating hate speech clauses serves a similar purpose.

In your attempt to determine what you can and cannot say, from not only a legal perspective, but a common decency perspective, a little common sense can go a long way. For instance, if there are words or terms that I know may be offensive or hurtful to someone, then I won't use those words. Why should I inflict intentional harm?

Whoever developed the saying, "Sticks and stones may break my bones, but names will never hurt me," was naïve. Rather, I subscribe to the statement, "Sticks and stones may break my bones, but words can scar a lifetime," All of us can recall being ridiculed as kids or being insulted as adults, and those words are not easily forgotten. Words are a most powerful weapon. They are how wars are literally started and ended. If by changing my vocabulary to avoid causing harm I am to be judged as being "politically correct," then I am most certainly guilty.

However, getting caught up in terminology or over analyzing what you say before you say it, can cause well-intentioned people to become overly cautious. Censoring everything you think and feel results in our conversations becoming less genuine.

For example, Santa's in Australia were told to refrain from using St. Nick's traditional "Ho Ho Ho" greeting because it was derogatory and offensive towards women. Santa Claus' were instructed instead to say "Ha Ha Ha." Is it any wonder why so many people get frustrated and discount the validity and importance of choosing our words wisely?

Yet that same term, "Ho" was used by Don Imus, a talk show host to describe Black athletes of the Rutgers University women's basketball team when he referred to them as "Nappy headed Ho's." The implication for using "Ho" in that context is far more offensive than Santa's simple greeting of "Ho Ho Ho."

What's the answer? Sometimes we need to reach around the words in order to balance our humanity with our individual freedoms. We also need to recognize that there is power in our words and how we choose to use them. Words are the vehicle through which communication is exchanged and reflect how we see our world and those around us. What you say matters. The question becomes, are you willing to improve your impact on others?

A WORD ABOUT WORDS

Have you ever found yourself unsure of what to say, or what word to use, so said nothing? One of the major challenges when communicating across differences centers on the use of language and terminology. Words can ease your ability to communicate or they can put up walls, often without your awareness. And, to add more confusion, the meanings of words change along with the times. What was once accepted terminology is no longer acceptable. What was once funny is now potentially offensive.

Staying current on appropriate word choice and phrases requires effort on your part. Unfortunately, we don't receive daily email updates with advice on today's acceptable language. Often the updating of language is done through personal trial and error which can be frustrating and embarrassing. Some unintentional mistakes in language are met with judgment and impatience. People on the receiving end of this exchange are tired of having to constantly serve as educators, with the expectation that they must be patient with the person who is using language that they find offensive. And conversely, people whose language is being corrected are tired of being educated, and believe that too much emphasis is placed on words and people are overreacting.

For instance, decades ago the term "colored people" was regarded as a polite description of black people. Nowadays, this term is seen as offensive and has been replaced with the term "people of color." This terminology is used to describe all non-white people, not just black people. The emphasis is on the person and not on the color.

"Mulatto" was another common term that was used many years ago to describe people who we would now refer to as biracial or multiracial. This term is thought to be derived from the word mulatto (small mule), which itself is derived from mulo (mule), once a generic name of any hybrid species.

"Oriental" is no longer seen as a welcomed term to describe people. The term is associated with foreign or exotic objects and is used as an adjective to describe an object such as a rug or vase. However, used as a noun, the word objectifies and demeans people from Asia or of Asian decent. "Oriental" continues to be descriptive of many things, but is best not to be used to describe people.

Adding to the confusion, sometimes terminology which once was offensive is now acceptable. As a means of empowerment, a group or political movement may "take back" a word to diminish its negative impact. "Queer" is now an acceptable term by those in the queer movement. Queer studies is now a discipline being offered at colleges and universities, yet at the same time the use of this word can be a slippery slope. This relatively new acceptance of the word queer is favored in certain arenas and still taboo in others.

Within the disability movement, there are people who reclaimed the term "disabled" after it had fallen out of favor. The term had previously described the physical, developmental or psychological "impairments" of the person, and was experienced by many as disempowering. Reframing the word "disabled" places the focus on external barriers of accessibility and inequity. It is the barriers which are disabling rather than the person themselves. Others in the disability movement prefer the term "people with disabilities," as it places the focus on the person rather than the disability.

Similarly, the term "handicapped" is not viewed favorably by people with disabilities. Some believe that this word was developed because the person with the disability had to beg for money with their "cap" in "hand." This is a falsehood. What is true, however, is that people with disabilities have been, and continue to be, discriminated and excluded from the workforce.

So what do we do with all of this language shifting, short of not saying anything? Where there is no risk, there is no reward. Stretching out of your comfort zone by having dialogue with people who are different increases your opportunity to succeed. You wisely choose not to use profanity in your daily conversations as you know it offends others. This matters because profanity limits your effectiveness professionally and personally. Your reputation and image are blemished. Essentially you are sabotaging yourself. Many people experience your misuse of terminology as equally offensive. Therefore, you must take proper action which increases the quality of your vocabulary.

Your willingness to risk saying the wrong thing will be uncomfortable and embarrassing in the short term. Yet in the long term, the benefits far exceed the shorter term consequences. This risk taking is an essential element to your growth and building significant connections.

If you use a word that is no longer seen as acceptable, you may be judged as a bigot. On the other hand, if you are a person that offers suggestions to someone as to a more compassionate terminology, you are often seen as being politically correct and all of the negative judgments attached with the term are thrust upon you. Even the term politically correct is a relatively new term, created out of frustration by people who felt under fire by the constant updating of language, or by people who simply refuse to alter their language because they may view it as petty or as an assault on their personal liberty.

Here's an example of when I used a word that I had no idea was problematic, yet one of my black colleagues found offensive. During a meeting I used the word "blackmail." My black colleague asked me, "What did you say?" Thinking she did not hear me, I repeated my previous statement which still included the word "blackmail." Again she questioned me. She was not disrespectful, nor was she aggressive, yet I still did not understand what the problem was. Finally she said that she found the word to have racist connotations and suggested I use a different word in the future such as "coerced." Embarrassed and somewhat humiliated, I replaced the word "blackmail" with "coerced." That seemed to alleviate the problem and I continued on with my remarks.

For the remainder of the meeting I felt my humiliation beginning to well up inside me. I just did not understand what the big deal was and why she had to correct me in front of all of our colleagues.

But THIS became the critical moment of decision. I wondered, "Do I catch up with her at the end of the meeting and talk with her about it, or do I leave the meeting making assumptions and feeling unsettled?" The importance of making this decision cannot be overstated, for it is essential in making the bridge towards effective communication.

To finish this story, I did speak with her at the end of the meeting and to both of our credit, it was a very fruitful conversation which allowed us to have other such conversations in the future.

I learned that by understanding how people are impacted by words and statements clears the way for better communication, and dramatically increase your effectiveness as a leader.

Even though I continue to make naïve statements, which tend to alienate the very people I am trying to connect with, I have learned to respond in a more effective manner. I try not to fix it, negate it, make light of it, or pretend I didn't say it, in the hopes that they didn't hear me. This doesn't mean my attempts always work, but the odds are much better if I don't simply ignore the problem.

As we proceed to explore some of the most common statements which act as pitfalls to effective communication, bear in mind what your ultimate goal or outcome is that you want to achieve. If your ultimate goal is to build better connections with people of varying viewpoints, then this book will offer you effective strategies to be successful. If your goal is to be "right" or to "win" the debate, then your results will be very different. Too often we get stuck in trying to convince the other person of our perspective and that we are right. Of course, the stronger we try to convince them, the more likely they will get defensive or stop listening to us. Therefore, we should always start with the end in mind, which is to decide what we want our outcome to be and working backwards.

When it comes to doing the right thing, good intentions are not enough. However, just because we put our foot in our mouth on occasion, all is not lost. Building a set of skills by which to communicate will have a powerful effect on every relationship in your life. These skills or competencies are transferable to any conversation, with anyone, at any time. They are particularly helpful in dialogues around issues of diversity, given the sometimes volatile nature of these conversations. Following are some of the skills and core concepts which are critical for your success.

"Sometimes we are so afraid of saying the wrong things that we make the biggest mistake of all and say nothing."

MAURA J CULLEN

THE 10 CORE CONCEPTS

Chapter Two

Core Concept #1

INTENT VS IMPACT

Even well-intended people cause harm. As such, people will often make statements which they intend or perceive to be supportive or complimentary, yet end up becoming problematic.

Often these statements are made when we are experiencing some discomfort, or when we are trying very hard to let the other person know that we are a "good" person who "gets it." Meant as joining statements, these remarks often have the opposite effect and end up creating a larger divide, and at times even angering the other person. Unfortunately, many of us are not aware that we have done anything harmful.

The sooner we are able to understand the impact our words or actions have on others, the sooner we will transform the quality of our interactions. The worst possible way to react when we have caused harm is to become defensive or dismissive. Accepting responsibility for our mistakes is essential in building a positive connection.

One familiar way this concept shows up is when someone tells a joke or uses a particular word that the other person takes offense to. Many of us become defensive and even upset that the other person appears to be taking the joke personally when we didn't mean anything by it. We even take it one step further and say or think, "It was only a joke, lighten up!" This action ends up only upsetting the other person even more.

The first step in being willing to accept responsibility is to understand that even well-intended people can cause harm.

This concept is the cornerstone to initiating and sustaining successful and meaningful conversations. Just because we don't intend or mean to hurt someone with our words, doesn't mean it still doesn't do just that. Apologizing is a critical action step to take, it may lessen the hurt, but it still cannot take away the impact. Once a comment or action is put out there, it is impossible to reverse the process. By accepting responsibility for our actions, or at times lack of action, the healing process will begin much sooner.

Let's look at an example of Intent vs. Impact as it relates to race.

Perhaps the most common dumb statement well-intended white people say is, "Some of my best friends are Black, Latina, Asian, etc…" The intention of the white person is to let the person of color know that they have some experience with people of a different race. With this experience is the assumption that they know what it is like to be a member of that group that we fully understand the challenges and issues that people of color face. However, good intentions do not always translate into good outcomes.

The impact it may have on the person of color can be very frustrating. As hard as a white person may try to understand what it is like to be a person of color in this society, it is impossible to fully grasp the depth that race has on our society. For the person of color, hearing the statement may be experienced as, "Since some of my best friends are…then there is no way I can be racist."

One way that white people try to avoid the negative label of being racist is to focus on our intention. We think as long as we didn't intend to cause harm then we should be afforded the benefit of the doubt and forgiven. People of color, on the other hand, tend to focus on the impact it has on them. It is very difficult to give people the benefit of the doubt when they refuse to accept responsibility for their actions. The following example is an illustration of this concept.

If you were driving a car and took your eyes off the road for a moment (not hard to imagine in a world of cell phones and multi-tasking), and ran someone over, chances are you would say that you didn't intend to run them over, but rather you took your eyes off the road for a moment. You may even go so far as to try to blame the person who was hit, saying, "Where did you come from? You ran out of nowhere!" On the other hand, the person who was hit and is now under your car is most likely focusing on the impact of your careless behavior, which has ended in their being transported to the hospital.

As the person who was careless, there are several ways you could respond to this incident. One option is to blame the victim by suggesting that it was somehow their fault because they were not paying attention or being careful enough. Or you may try to shift the focus by saying that you did not intend to hurt them - that this was all a terrible accident. Yes, accidents do happen. However, most accidents occur because someone is being careless. Lastly, you could choose the option which takes responsibility for your carelessness, pick up the pieces and try to make things as right as possible.

"Think about everything you believe
but do not believe everything you think!"

Maura J Cullen

Core Concept #2

PILE ON PRINCIPLE (P.O.P.)

The *Pile On Principle* (*P.O.P.*) is critical in understanding why people sometimes overreact. It is easily demonstrated by the parent who loses their patience after the tenth time their child has asked the same question over and over again, despite the parent telling them to stop. For many, overreacting comes from the experience of being asked the same questions a multitude of times over a lifetime; these questions are outlined in the "35 Dumb Things Well-Intended People Say" section.

However, to truly demonstrate the power of *P.O.P*, let's take a look at a longer example. Say you get up in the morning on the proverbial "wrong side of the bed." The first thing you do is to stub your toe. Not a good start to the morning.

When you arrive at work, a colleague accidentally steps on the same foot you hurt that morning. They say they are sorry - they didn't mean to hurt you. Of course you accept their apology and tell them "No problem!" even though it hurts and you are frustrated. Just because they didn't intend to harm you doesn't mean it doesn't hurt (*Intent vs. Impact*). It still hurts!

Then, while meeting a friend for lunch that afternoon in a busy restaurant, the waiter accidentally drops a tray of food on that same foot. Now your foot hurts more than ever and you are about to lose control. You are angry and frustrated, but you don't want to freak out in public, so you limp out of the restaurant, quietly seething inside.

Now, in order to protect your foot from any further harm, you start to create more space between yourself and other people to avoid having someone else inadvertently stomp on your injured toe, as you are tired of experiencing pain.

As you arrive home from a long day, (with your foot still throbbing), you gratefully kick off your shoes and try to relax. Sensing that you have had a bad day, your partner brings you a cold drink. Unfortunately, as he hands you the drink, he accidentally brushes his shoe against your injured toe. All of a sudden, you shoot up in frustration, hurt and enraged, and begin to yell at your partner. It's as though your foot has a big bull's-eye target stamped on it that says "Step on me today." You are so tired of getting stepped on and being hurt all day long, that you end up taking it out on the person who has hurt you the least.

As you are going through the process of venting your frustration, your partner is looking at you like you've suddenly sprouted ten heads. He is thinking that he barely touched you and that you are overreacting. He begins to get defensive and somewhat annoyed with you. He has no idea of the events that have taken place over the course of your day. He only sees the snapshot of the moment he brushed against your foot. Yet if he had seen a video of the entire day and witnessed how often you were hurt, then he most likely would have more empathy for you.

That was one day in the life of your foot. Now imagine a lifetime of hurt being piled on hurt, of being told you're not good enough, or having derogatory words or jokes continually directed at you. In order to avoid some of this pain, many of us create barriers or distance between ourselves and others in an effort to save ourselves from incurring more pain. In real life, we usually only see snapshots of people's experience and base our perceptions on those one or two examples. The most important element to bear in mind is that we all have videos of our past experiences, and some of the not so positive ones can pile up, until one day we cry out in pain and frustration or lash out.

If you are the person who tells a joke that offends someone, or uses a word that annoys another, remember that you are only seeing a "snapshot" of this person. It is very likely that there is a long video history of pain that has been piled too high for too long and they are finally reacting now. Instead of getting defensive and criticizing the person for overreacting, demonstrating empathy will likely deescalate their frustration and increase the probability of a connection with that person.

Here is a more concrete example which demonstrates this process. Let's take the experience of a Latina woman. She grew up hearing many derogatory words about Latinos and

Hispanics, many of which were directed at her. In high school, her white guidance counselor suggested that she take classes to learn a skill so that she could get a job right after high school. He never raised the possibility of her going to college. Despite his lack of encouragement and support, she attends college on an academic scholarship.

After graduation, she gets a job and during her first week hears remarks that she was hired to fill a "quota." Later that week, her boss calls her into the office and tells her to refrain from speaking Spanish at work because it makes non-Spanish speakers feel uncomfortable. As she heads back to her desk she overhears a couple of her co-workers telling some racial jokes. Things are piling up quickly. She calls a friend to meet her after work to have coffee so that she can vent some of her frustrations. As she walks to the table at the restaurant, another customer assumes she is a waitress and asks for more water. Bad day? Perhaps. An unusual day for a Latina? Perhaps not.

Core Concept #3

EXPLAIN AWAYS

When people come to you with a problem, it is instinctual to try and fix it. After all, why else would they be sharing this

"Some people want to learn things they do not know, while others do not wish to know the things they have learned."

MAURA J CULLEN

problem with you? In your attempt to fix the problem however, you may inadvertently be adding to it.

Have you ever had the experience of speaking with someone and the only expectation you had was to vent? You didn't want them to fix the problem, negate it or explain it - you just wanted them to listen. Their attempts to fix it or explain it away often has an adverse effect on you which increases your frustration. It's as though they don't believe we are capable of resolving our own problems. This is just another example of a well-intended person wanting to help, but having a negative impact. Here's an example of an *explain away*.

Car dealers are notorious for treating female customers as second class citizens. Personally, I have had the displeasure of such an experience when I have gone to buy a new car. Typically when a customer comes onto a car lot, a salesperson is quick to greet them as most salespeople are paid by commission.

After much research, I went to three different car dealerships to test drive the cars I was interested in purchasing. Purposely, I had decided to go during the week in order to avoid the weekend rush of customers. When I arrived at the first lot, not one salesperson came to greet me even though I was the only customer there at the time. After fifteen minutes had passed, I decided to go in to speak with a salesperson. Immediately I noticed four men (all who were salespeople), standing around chatting and drinking coffee. They were strategically positioned near the window so that they would be able to monitor the car lot as new customers came in, so it is a good bet that they saw me enter the lot. As I entered the showroom area, I still did not receive any acknowledgment or service. Finally, I had to interrupt their conversation in order to have some of my questions addressed.

A similar experience happened at one of the other dealerships as well. (This is also an example of P.O.P (*Pile On Principle*). Because I felt mistreated at the first dealership, I was a bit more hesitant when I went to the next dealership, concerned that I might be mistreated again. When the same thing did happen, I was even more agitated than the first time it occurred. By the time I arrived at the third dealership, I felt almost certain that I would be mistreated once again. As a result, I was very cautious and did not trust that I would be treated with respect.

Thankfully, at the third dealership I had a very different and positive experience. It should be noted here that I ended up buying my car at the third dealership. Never would I have purchased my car at either of the first two dealerships after the treatment I received. Not understanding these core concepts of *intent/impact* and the *Pile On Principle*, cost those salesmen their commission.

Customers are very loyal to those who serve them well and treat them with respect, and tend to tell others about the positive experience they've had dealing with these specific companies or businesses.

When my car shopping expedition was complete, I described my experience to two of my friends - one man and one woman. Immediately, the woman began nodding her head in affirmation and letting me know that she understood my experience. This was very comforting to me as it validated how I was feeling.

My male friend had a very different reaction, a more defensive posture. He tried to rationalize and *explain away* why my experience had nothing to do with gender. I cannot speak to his intent, whether it was to *explain away* the salesmen's behavior, or to eliminate the possibility of sexism in order to make me feel better. Regardless, his reaction made me feel dismissed and belittled.

The key to this dynamic is not the *intent*, but rather the *impact*. Is it possible that everything that happened to me could be explained by factors other than the sexism? Absolutely. It could be explained away in a number of ways. Perhaps the men were all out back and didn't see me come onto the lot. Maybe they had been dealing with customers on the phone and just finished their calls as I entered the showroom. Or even still, maybe they weren't ignoring me because I was a woman; they may have made assumptions on the way I was dressed that I could not afford one of their cars. Any of these reasons are plausible. Is it also possible that they responded the way they did out of sexism? Absolutely.

Instead of trying to *explain away* my experience at the dealership, a better approach my male friend could have taken was to simply acknowledge what had happened to me. Both my female friend and I would have been better served if he had said something like, "That must have been frustrating" or "Has a similar thing like that happened to you before?" Bear in mind that acknowledging my experience did not mean that he had to agree with it. When people are put into the position of having to legitimize their experiences, the divide continues to widen. Instead of offering possible explanations or solutions, it's best if you let them talk... and you listen. One of the best ways to reduce our frustration is to have someone listen to us without them trying to fix it.

Core Concept #4

IN-GROUP/OUT-GROUP LANGUAGE

We often get confused as to why some people can use derogatory words or jokes and it is acceptable, while others who say exactly the same thing are judged and receive negative reactions. The answer is easy. If you are not a member of the group being described by the derogatory words, then it is best not to use it! We could get into the debate as to whether or not

*"Sticks and stones may break my bones
but words can scar a lifetime."*

MAURA J CULLEN

this is fair, but you would be wasting your breath. Fair or not, it is what it is. Let's look at a familiar example.

For those of you who have siblings, this analogy will be especially easy. Let's say that you are using negative adjectives about one of your siblings to a friend - about how your brother or sister is this or that. The next day, that friend uses the very same words about your sibling that you had. Now how do you respond? For many, we tend to get defensive and angry at our friend. How dare they say that about my sibling! Who do they think they are? You, like many, might get defensive and angry at your friend. All of a sudden you become your siblings' strongest advocate. You chastise your friend and they haven't any idea of what they have done. After all, they are using the very same words that you had used the day before. The difference? There seems to be an unspoken rule about this. As long as you are within the "group," you can get away with saying what you want. If you are outside the group, just don't go there.

An example of *In-Group/Out-Group* language is the use of the terms "fag" and "dyke." Both of these words are used in the gay, lesbian, bisexual and transgender (GLBT) communities with little controversy. By adopting a more positive slant on the words, the GLBT community's intent is to reclaim their own power which these words were created to thwart.

When heterosexuals use these terms, they are seen by GLBT people as still having the negative historical perspective which heterosexuals created. Even if heterosexuals have friends who are GLBT and don't mind them using "fag" and "dyke", it is best to refrain. You never know who else might be listening or how it may be taken.

Core Concept #5

ADVANTAGED AND DISADVANTAGED GROUP IDENTITIES

Many different terms are used to describe the dynamics of *advantaged* and disadvantaged groups. Some of the other terms used to describe *advantaged* groups are: dominant, privileged, oppressor and majority. Some terms used to describe *disadvantaged* groups are: subordinate, target, oppressed and minority. For the purposes of this book, I will be using the terms *advantaged* and *disadvantaged*, as it speaks to the dynamics of difference and inequality in a very simple and straightforward manner.

The concept of *advantaged/disadvantaged* is simple, yet the dynamics are complicated. For the most part we have very little, if any, control over our status as *advantaged* or

"You don't always get rewarded for doing what is right. In fact, at times we get rewarded for doing what is wrong."

MAURA J CULLEN

disadvantaged. It is not so much a "blame game" as it is a "name game." Meaning that whatever group you have been named or identified as, will determine some of your status in the power and privilege pecking order we call life. The thing about privilege is that those who have it did nothing to earn it. Privilege is given as a result of your group membership, and having this membership gives them an advantage over others. In order to fully grasp the roots of oppression and privilege and why there is so much adversity when talking of diversity, this concept must be understood.

People in the *advantaged* groups are institutionally and culturally in power. People in the *disadvantaged* groups do not have that same power and privilege, institutionally and culturally. This is not to suggest *disadvantaged* people are not powerful people. In fact, the saying, "What doesn't break us makes us stronger" is often an accurate saying for people in these groups.

In order to demonstrate the concept of *Advantaged/Disadvantaged* groups, I've compiled an abbreviated list of categories. There are many more groups beyond the ones I mention here.

Race:

White people are *Advantaged*

People of Color are *Disadvantaged*

Gender:

Men are *Advantaged*

Women and Transgender People are *Disadvantaged*

Religion:

Christians are *Advantaged*

Non-Christians are *Disadvantaged*

Sexual Orientation:

Heterosexuals are *Advantaged*

Gays, lesbians, bisexuals are *Disadvantaged*

Age:

Middle-aged people are *Advantaged*

Young and very old are *Disadvantaged*

Socio-economic class:

Middle to Upper class people are *Advantaged*

Poor or working class people are *Disadvantaged*

Ability:

Able-bodied people are *Advantaged*

People with Disabilities are *Disadvantaged*

"Diversity training takes good people and makes them better. Yet being a good person is not enough. You need skills and awareness to make a significant positive impact."

MAURA J CULLEN

Core Concept #6

PRIVILEGE

In terms of a definition, privilege can best be described as access to resources based solely on the person's status as a member of the *advantaged* group. *Privilege* is a concept that many people in *advantaged* groups have difficulty understanding or accepting. A common reaction is to become defensive and feel they are being categorized unfairly. It's as though they are being accused of cheating when they haven't done anything wrong. Privilege is given, not earned. It is distributed based on what group a person belongs to, rather than what they have or have not accomplished. One of my favorite quotes is by Barry Switzer who says, "Some people are born on third base and go through life thinking they've hit a triple." People in *advantaged* groups need to be reminded that they have been given a head start, that their journey begins on third base without even taking a swing. Whether or not they asked for this head start is irrelevant - they have it. What matters most is what they do with their privilege.

Let me give you a couple of examples. The first example speaks to white privilege. Many white people often say that they have earned everything they achieved in their lives, without acknowledging that they have been given a bit of a "racial head start" or advantage so to speak. This is not to discount the accomplishments that many white people have worked hard for, but simply believing that they have earned everything without acknowledging the benefits given by the mere fact they are white is naïve.

Here is a list of privileges that white people experience often without knowing:

- White people can be hired for a job and not be accused of getting it because of a "quota."

- White people can make mistakes and not have it serve as an example as to why their entire race is not competent.

- White people can go shopping and be assured that they will not be followed because of their color or because they are thought to be a shoplifter.

- White people won't hesitate to call police for assistance. Police are seen as helpful and will likely believe their account of a situation. Police are not viewed as a threat to their safety.

- White history, otherwise known as "history," is taught at every level at every school in this country.

- White people can go to most any store and find hair care products, band aids, cosmetics, etc. to match their skin color.

Another example of privilege is heterosexual privilege and the institution of marriage. With the exception of the states of Massachusetts and California, only heterosexual couples can be legally married. They don't have to "do" anything but be heterosexual, and they automatically gain the privilege of marriage, with all of the legal rights and benefits associated with that institution. Married heterosexual couples are automatically given many legal rights such as spousal health insurance, recipient of a spouse's pension plan, ability to visit a spouse in the hospital when visitation is limited to only "family" members, tax benefits, ability to adopt children without regard to sexual orientation, discounts on memberships to fitness clubs etc. The list goes on and on.

Not only are there legal privileges and benefits, there is the issue of social acceptance as well. Society builds entire industries to support and encourage heterosexual marriages. From wedding planning, shower registries, honeymoon destinations, to the assurance that you can introduce a loved one to family members without fear of rejection, are a few of the distinctions heterosexuals enjoy. Simply purchasing a greeting card for a loved one becomes a challenging task for gay and lesbian couples because the wording and pictures on the card are composed for heterosexuals.

"Consistency of behavior can ultimately be unfair."

MAURA J CULLEN

Core Concept #7

BEING CONSISTENT IS NOT ALWAYS FAIR

Let me pose this question: In order to be fair, does one need to be consistent? I recall having my first meeting with a new work group where I had asked them to create a list of values they would like to see in a supervisor. On that list were the words fair and consistent. After some thought, I said to the group that sometimes being fair and consistent are one and the same. However, there are also times when the two concepts will be competing. For example, in order to be fair to all those involved, it might mean that I would not be consistent in my response. This concept can strike quite a bit of adversity when discussing issues of diversity and difference. Is it fair to treat people differently? This thought process led to a very helpful and insightful conversation which guided some of our values and expectations of one another in the year which followed.

Let's look at an example. Say you and some friends go out to eat. When the bill arrives, someone suggests that to make it easier you should split the bill evenly among all of you. This is definitely consistent, but is it fair? What if your meal only cost $10, and your friends' meals and their drinks total between $20-$30 each? In this scenario it would not be fair to expect everyone to pay the same amount. Fairness in this case would mean treating people differently.

AFFIRMATIVE ACTION

One of the more contentious topics when discussing issues of diversity is Affirmative Action. This phrase was first introduced in 1961 by President John F. Kennedy when he created the committee on Equal Employment Opportunity. It mandated that federally funded projects need to take "Affirmative Action," ensuring hiring and employment practices are free from racial bias. In 1965, President Lyndon Johnson signed Executive Order 11246, enforcing Affirmative Action policy. This was later amended in 1967 to include gender bias as well. In theory, adhering to this policy would create equal access to opportunity for all.

How these goals were, and still are implemented today, take many forms. One common way is in the informal practice of quotas. Filling quotas was never the intent nor the letter of the law for Affirmative Action. However, some people use the terms interchangeably.

Opponents of Affirmative Action will state that it is both an unfair and unwise practice - one that advances people not on merit but by identity. They argue that the ultimate goals of diversity objectives are to provide people with equal access without bias and prejudice. The notion of Affirmative Action, in their opinion, is doing just that - gaining an unfair advantage at the expense of others. Many white men may feel that they are the ones whose opportunities are sacrificed in this push for diversity.

On the other hand, people who support Affirmative Action believe that unless the status quo is challenged, nothing will change; that the informal practice of nepotism, which has become the standard, will continue to exist. This practice, many will state, is the practice of white men hiring a disproportionate number of other white men, or at times white women. In order to level the playing field and provide equal access and opportunity to all, everyone should be afforded the chance to compete. Affirmative Action is a way to hire the most talented and competent people who otherwise might be overlooked or ignored. It is also a vehicle to attract a diverse workforce with many backgrounds and varying perspectives.

Core Concept #8

ALLIES

An ally is a member of the *advantaged* group who takes action against injustice with the belief that all will benefit, not just those from *disadvantaged* groups. Being an ally is often easier said than done. It is a continual process of challenging common practices and beliefs. Being an ally takes fortitude and a willingness to right the wrongs of injustice.

*"Most times knowing what is right is the easy part;
it is in the doing that tests our courage."*

MAURA J CULLEN

There are many ways for people to demonstrate their power as an ally. Participating in a protest or march, confronting derogatory remarks or jokes, acknowledging and identifying unjust practices, donating money to certain causes or organizations, writing an article or a letter to the editor, and furthering your self-education are a few examples. Less assertive ways would include not laughing at derogatory jokes or comments and even walking away from the group. This can also be a powerful statement.

Examples of ally behavior includes someone without a disability working towards accessibility issues; men organizing a group to eliminate rape and sexual assault, or a white person challenging a racist joke or comment.

Recently I returned from a training seminar where I demonstrated the very pitfalls described in this book that I want people to avoid. During the course of this three day retreat, I stepped into some of the traps which I am sharing with you now. After the seminar was over, I felt sad and regretful that I did not respond the way I would have liked.

In this instance, a white man was using an *explain away* with a woman of color, trying to convince her that an experience she was describing had nothing to do with her racial identity. This led to the woman of color having to defend and legitimize her own experience - not a fun position for her to be placed, but often a familiar one. As the seminar facilitator, I failed to intervene which left a negative impact on some of the people of color. From their perspective, I was just another white person who is "supposed to get it," but didn't speak up and left it to the people of color to do the educating. This is a frequent occurrence that people from the *disadvantaged* groups experience and one which decreases levels of trust between people of color and whites.

One of my colleagues, a man of color, who was also in the training seminar, confronted me later about my silence and lack of action. He was frustrated and disappointed that I did not intervene as a white ally. Of course I felt terrible. I wanted to *explain away* what I had done so that he would cut me some slack. Yet that would have made an already bad situation worse. So I merely sat there, wishing it were all over so that I could return to the safety of my hotel room.

When I returned to my hotel room, I was angry; not only at myself, but at the people of color as well. My thought process included things like, "What do "they" want from me? At least I am a white person who is trying to make things right, but still I get criticized." It felt like no matter what I did or didn't do, I could never get it right. A part of me wanted to say, "I give up! Why should I even bother trying if all I am going to get in return is grief?" But that is the point. I was looking for them to give me something in return, perhaps a pat on the back, an appreciative smile, a simple acknowledgement. Here's the thing: if we only try to do the right thing when we're sure to receive praise for it, then there will be many experiences when we don't take the right action. As a result we end up being ineffective in our efforts to level the playing field. The challenge becomes doing the right thing even when others don't reward us.

Here's an illustration. Imagine you are driving your car and you come upon a crosswalk with people wanting to cross the street. The rule of the road says that we must stop our car and let the people cross as they have the right away. But the thing is this: you are in a car which is a very powerful deterrent to people who want to cross. You think you are doing the right thing by stopping and allowing them to cross. You believe you deserve a smile or a hand wave as appreciation for your thoughtfulness. However, they neglect to thank you. Do you run them over when they are at the half-way point of the crosswalk?

Being a member of *advantaged* groups is like being the driver of the car. You have lots of power and control that could determine other people's experience.

Being an ally can be an unpredictable and bumpy road, filled with uncertainty. One thing that you can be certain of is that as an ally you WILL make mistakes; you will disappoint yourself at times and disappoint others as well. It is not a role for the meek. Being an ally is like seeking perfection in an imperfect world.

Given everything I have described in this section, why in the world would anyone want to be an ally? There are many ways to respond to this question and it differs for every person. For me, it means maintaining my sense of integrity. The consequences of not being one far outweigh the hassles of doing my best to be a good ally. An ally is someone people can count on not necessarily to always get it right, but someone who cares enough to hang in there when the going gets tough.

Basically it boils down to this: if people are willing to mistreat and discriminate against one group of people, it is just a matter of time before this mistreatment gets to you. Therefore, it is in your best interest to help eradicate prejudice and inequity when you witness it. Taking immediate action disrupts the cycle of ignorance and bigotry.

Core Concept #9
RAISING THE B.A.R.

One of the most powerful tools I have found in dealing with events or conversations about diversity is the acronym **B.A.R.** I wanted to create a simple yet effective way to deal with my emotions when someone was doing or saying things that I found offensive. In the past I would get very angry at what someone was saying or doing and immediately react, which was not always the best course of action. It was the old adage of "open-mouth-insert-foot," so I developed this term that I like to think of as "**Raising the B.A.R.**" The concept may be simple, but do not underestimate the power it has when you put it into action.

What follows is a description of two very different models of communication. The first, **B.A.R.**, is the more desirable of the two as it creates a respectful and more compassionate exchange. The second model, **R.A.B.** (**B.A.R.** in reverse) is an ineffective and harmful mode of communication.

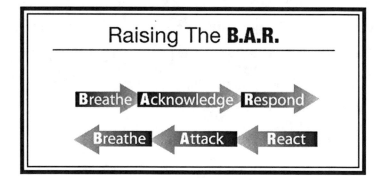

B. The letter "B" in **B.A.R.**, reminds us to *Breathe* when we get into stressful situations. Breathing is one of the most effective, but underutilized tools available. As you sit here reading this, I invite you to take a deep breath.

"When dealing with anger and frustration we often choose between imploding and exploding our emotions. Neither is a wise decision."

MAURA J CULLEN

I mean it. Please take a deep breath. When we do this it serves several purposes.

1. It relaxes us, which is always a good way to approach a stressful conversation.

2. It sends oxygen to our brains which also serves us well.

3. It buys us some time so that we can choose a better response.

4. Most important we cannot speak when we are trying to breathe. This saves us from the "open mouth - insert foot" drama.

A. The letter "**A**" in **B.A.R.**, suggests that we *Acknowledge* what the other person is saying. Vital to your success in achieving this challenging goal is to understand one very important distinction. In order to acknowledge what someone else is saying, you do not have to agree with them.

Acknowledging can be actively listening and repeating back to the person what they are saying, to make certain that you fully understand what they mean. You may also ask clarifying questions or ask them to give you some examples. Ask them how they arrived at such a conclusion. The most important part of this stage is that the other person feels as though they have been heard and that you understand. It does not necessarily mean you agree with what they are trying to communicate.

R. The letter **"R"** in **B.A.R.**, has us *Responding* to the other person. Notice that this is the last step in a three stage process, not the first step which usually occurs in our conversations. Making it the final stage and not the first, you accomplish two things. The first is the notion of "seek first to understand before being understood." The beauty of this is that once a person gets a chance to speak their mind and feel understood, they are more likely to listen to what you have to say. Secondly, we are able to formulate a better response given this understanding and are less reactionary.

In our less than perfect moments as human beings, we sometimes do this process in reverse, bringing about a very different result. Instead of doing **B.A.R.**, we do **R.A.B.** Here is the three step process in reverse showing the exact opposite result of what we're trying to achieve.

R. Instead of Responding, we React. There are many times in our lives when reacting is a very good thing, such as moving your hand away from a hot stove or ducking when an object is coming at you. Being in the middle of a heated discussion is not one of those times. Many of us have had the experience of saying something out of reaction without giving it any thought, and have come to regret that choice. The major difference between Responding and Reaction is thought. A decision based out of thought will almost always be the better choice. The reason why it is essential to breathe as a first step is that it buys you time to formulate one coherent thought. As I have already mentioned, when you take a deep intentional breath it is impossible to speak, thereby saving you from saying something you might regret.

A. Instead of Acknowledging, we Attack. When we don't like what the other person is saying, we take offense and go on the attack. Sometimes we make a personal attack on the person or we attack what they are saying. Either way, the other person is unlikely to respond favorably to what you have said. This is the step which usually gets us into trouble. We get so caught up in our emotions that we feel as though we have little control over what we say, as if our words are on automatic pilot. The truth is that we do have control, and choosing to go on the attack is almost always a bad choice.

B. After all of the energy we have just spent on reacting and attacking we need to Breathe. It is not like the deep cleansing breath we took in the other approach, rather the kind of breath that a fighter takes in between boxing rounds. It's as though we are catching our breath quickly so that the other person cannot get their say.

Here's an illustration. I was conducting a day long diversity seminar and one of the participants took offense that I am lesbian. He shared with the group his religious convictions and stated that I was a sinner and was going to hell (this is the abbreviated version). This caught people's attention and the room seemed to have stopped breathing as they waited for my response. There was a time in my life when I would have reacted very strongly to him, accusing him of being a hypocrite, and asking him who was he to judge people? I probably would have gone on to say that he was the one going to hell and whatever else I could shout at him before I needed to take another breath. Truth be told, there are some days that I still might be tempted to react in an aggressive and judgmental manner, as it is very frustrating to be continually discriminated against. From having my home and cars damaged to receiving death threats, the *Pile On Principle* could have me responding in ways I would rather not.

On that day, in that moment, with that person, I must have done something right, because despite our obvious disagreements we were still able to manage a meaningful exchange. As he was making his comments to me, I immediately began taking some deep breaths to calm myself. When he was done talking, I asked him if I could ask a couple of clarifying questions. Then I acknowledged what courage it took for him to say what he said. I continued to acknowledge that he was not the first or the last person in the world to have those beliefs, that I grew up hearing some of those same comments and understood how he came to those conclusions. I also acknowledged that his comments and perspective were an important part of this experience. Once I felt I had done a good job of acknowledging his position, I gave my response. I told him that as passionate and proud he was of his religious identity, I was equally passionate and proud of who and what I am, and that our positions could not be further apart from one another. I shared with him and the group the impact of having comments like those directed towards me and other gay people and the toll it takes on all of us.

At the next break during the seminar, he came to thank me for treating him with respect and for not ridiculing him or his beliefs. It was then that I reflected on the previous interaction with him and created the elements which let to this successful exchange - Breathe, Acknowledge, Respond.

"At times we do the right thing for the wrong reasons, and other times we do the wrong thing for the right reasons."

MAURA J CULLEN

Core Concept #10
BYSTANDER BEHAVIOR

Sir Edmund Burke stated, "The only thing necessary for evil to triumph is for good people to do nothing." Perhaps there is no better quote than this to illustrate *Bystander Behavior*. The concept is very easy to understand, but avoiding its clutches is very different. Most of us have had the experience of witnessing someone being mistreated or ridiculed and doing absolutely nothing. We stood there and watched it happen. Too often I have felt guilty or ashamed that I did not respond in a manner that I could be proud of. I have come to know however, that my lack of action is an action in and of itself.

Where *bystander behavior* is the most challenging is with family and friends. It is much easier at times to challenge a stranger, but far more intimidating to challenge people we love or people with whom we work. There is more on the line and far more to risk. As a result, we are tempted to just to let their derogatory remarks or jokes slide by without comment from us.

Perhaps our reason for not taking action is the fear, real and/or perceived, of being fired from our job, losing a promotion or not being liked. Not being liked is a more common fear than people may admit. They don't want to say anything to alienate others, and the truth is we all like to be liked.

There are a host of reasons which influence our decision not to take action and some of them are more "legitimate" than others. There will be times that not taking action is the wiser course. For instance, if taking action would put you in harms way, or if you think your intervention would be more productive at another time, then it's best to consider an alternate plan. Sometimes we don't do anything because we do not know what it is that we should do. An example of this is when we see an adult chastising a child or being too rough with them. We know it is wrong and we want to stop it, but we don't know how to do it, or we may not feel as though it is our role to intervene. Another reason may be the moment passed so quickly, that by the time we got over our shock of what had been said or done, it was too late to do anything.

The reason that prevents many of us from taking action is fear. We risk so much when we stick our necks out - our jobs, our friends, how others view us, etc., so we let the moment pass without leaving our mark, or at least not one we are ultimately proud of. We might find ourselves offering *explain aways* as to why we decided not to take action. Often we are too afraid to do what we know in our heart is right. Most times knowing what is right is the easy part; it is the doing that tests our courage.

There are consequences for everything we do or don't do in life. Have you ever been on the other end and have been the one being ridiculed or mistreated? Perhaps there were some people whom you thought you could count on to "cover your back," but when push came to shove and it was time for them to show what they were made of, they remained silent and left you out there by yourself. Betrayal is a lousy lesson to learn, but it is the very byproduct of bystander behavior. Once someone has betrayed your trust, it takes time to rebuild that level of trust again.

There is far too much *bystander behavior* with issues of social justice and diversity. It's not a matter of people not caring - most people do care - but rather a matter of finding the courage and the time to take action despite some of the consequences.

Now that we understand some of the core concepts in building a solid foundation towards competency, let's look at some of the statements which well-intended people say that may inadvertently cause harm. Most all of us have said many of these statements at some point in our lives without knowing why they were hurtful or offensive. As we break down each of the pitfalls, we will look at the intention of the person saying the statement and what they are trying to convey to the other person.

Breaking down the statements in this manner will serve as a constant reminder of two of the critical core concepts; *Intent vs. Impact* and *P.O.P. (Pile On Principle)*. In an effort to make this process of successful communication automatic, we must continually ask ourselves how these 10 Core Concepts can enhance our interactions and then take action. We will also look at how these statements impact the other person and the best bet of what might be a better way to connect.

"A leader without ethics is like a boat without a rudder, their decisions determined by whichever way the wind blows."

MAURA J CULLEN

THE 35 DUMB THINGS WELL-INTENDED PEOPLE SAY

Chapter Three

1. "SOME OF MY BEST FRIENDS ARE... (Black, Gay, Muslim, Asian, etc...)"

INTENTION

The intention is to let the other person know that we have some personal experience with people from other group memberships like themselves. It is meant to make the other person feel comfortable, to build rapport and credibility.

IMPACT

This statement will almost always solicit a roll of the eyes. So what if some of your friends are (fill in the blank)? It feels as though you are showing a membership card for a group of which you are not a member. Just because you know someone who has a disability, doesn't mean you know everything there is to know about all people with disabilities. Nor should it suggest that your friends' experience is the same as the person with whom you are speaking. As soon as you make that remark, the person who is receiving the comment will most likely be offended and sincerely doubt that you do indeed have such friends.

BEST BET

Don't try so hard. Speak of your friends as it is appropriate, not as a way to gain points. It is also wise to stay away from a line which will cause similar reactions; "My friend, who HAPPENS to be…"

2. "I KNOW EXACTLY HOW YOU FEEL!"

INTENTION

This comment is used to find some common ground and to demonstrate your empathy and compassion to the other person. It is meant to lessen the other person's isolation by "normalizing" her/his experience.

IMPACT

This will typically shut the other person down for one very simple reason; you cannot know exactly how anyone else feels. Yes, perhaps you have had a similar experience, but right then the conversation is not about you, it is about them. Telling a wheelchair user that you know exactly how they feel because you used a wheelchair for a month due to an injury minimizes their daily experience.

BEST BET

Instead of saying "I know exactly how you feel," you might have more success if you ask them questions to further clarify their experience, or to simply acknowledge the feelings they are expressing. At some point you may join them with an example of when something similar happened to you, but always do this AFTER they have had enough time to talk about themselves first.

3. "I DON'T THINK OF YOU AS..."

INTENTION

We are attempting to suggest that this particular part of their identity does not influence our judgment of them, and that we are not prejudiced. We are trying to say that despite this difference, we will treat them the same, no matter what. It is important that we are perceived as fair and without bias.

IMPACT

The impact of this statement is that the person ends up feeling marginalized. Though well-intended, this statement implies that despite their being (fill in blank), you still accept them or like them. Imagine saying to a man, "I don't think of you as a man" - that is just plain silly. How is he to respond? Should he say "If you don't see me as a man, than just what do you see me as?" Of course you think of him as a man and why shouldn't you? After all, he is a man!

BEST BET

It is best not to discount significant parts of people's identities. Making the statement, "I don't think of you as…" is a contradiction, for in order to make that statement you had to think of them exactly in that way. Best bet is to realize that you do think of them as "…" and it is okay. There is no need to say otherwise, especially to that person. Noticing difference is natural. It is the action we take once we notice the difference that requires our mindfulness.

4. "THE SAME THING HAPPENS TO ME TOO."

INTENTION

By making this statement, we are trying to build an instant connection and bond. "The same thing happens to me" statement puts us both on the same team, with a joint understanding and shared experience.

IMPACT

So what if the same thing happened to you? Again, we are not talking about you right now. The impact of this statement is that the focus of the conversation shifts from them to you. It is a conversation stopper. You have interrupted their story and thus lost your chance to make the connection with them.

Besides, even though a similar thing may have happened to you, it does not mean it happened in the same way, or for the same reason, or to the same extent.

Let's expand the example of Core Concept #2, the *Pile On Principle*, to understand this dumb statement more clearly. That example describes the hurt and frustration of a person whose foot was stepped on repeatedly during the course of a day and the toll it took on them. Now imagine another person who has the same exact experience over the course of the day. However, unlike the first person, this individual has a broken foot. Even though you both experienced being stepped on, the pain is more excruciating for the person who came into the situation already having been hurt with a broken foot.

Here's another example. When a white person tells someone of Arab descent that they too get searched at airports, there is no acknowledgement that it probably happens more often to people of Arab descent, especially since 9/11. It probably not only happens more often, but most likely is based on their racial identity. By saying it also happens to you suggests that the reason it may happen to them has nothing to do with their racial identity. Is this a possibility? Certainly. There is also a good probability that it has everything to do with them being Arab. In addition, chances are this is not the first time it has happened to them, and that it is a common occurrence.

BEST BET

Listen to their story fully without interruption. Ask if this has happened to them before. Try to keep the focus on them and not shift it to you. At some point later in the conversation, you might offer that a similar thing happened to you and how it made you feel. However, it is important to note the difference of the impact due to group membership as opposed to individual experience. Remember, the outcome you want is to join them with a common experience, not "topping" their story with a "better" one or minimizing their experience with an *explain away*.

Never underestimate the power of active listening; of being fully engaged in what the other person is telling you. Just listening without judgment is an effective tool to building rapport.

5. "IT WAS ONLY A JOKE! DON'T TAKE THINGS SO SERIOUSLY."

INTENTION

When people use this statement they are often attempting to lighten up a tense situation by using humor following an inappropriate remark or joke.

IMPACT

You may as well tell them to shut up because it has the same effect. It's a "double whammy." First, you make an inappropriate remark or joke which the person finds offensive. Second, when the person responds in a serious manner or confronts you, you then end up insulting them again for not laughing at your ignorance, by telling them not to take things so seriously. When men make sexist remarks and then follow it by blaming a woman's reaction on "that time of the month," it sets into motion the concept of P.O.P. and the process starts all over again.

BEST BET

When it is clear that the other person has been offended by your joke, don't go on the defensive. Perhaps saying you are sorry is a good start. It is best not to complicate matters by suggesting that they just "lighten up."

6. "WHAT DO 'YOUR' PEOPLE THINK?"

INTENTION

The intent of this statement is seeking information about a group of people with whom you may not be familiar or not know much about in regards to their culture or experiences.

IMPACT

This evokes the "If you've seen one, you've seen them all" feeling. It is one of the more obvious forms of stereotyping. When O.J. Simpson was on trial for the murders of his wife Nicole and Ron Goldman, many black people reported being frequently asked by white people, "What do YOUR people think?" It's as if because they are black they had the inside scoop as to O.J.'s guilt or innocence. This suggests that there is one cohesive response to what millions of people think. This singling out is also common in predominately white classrooms and workplaces. It is not uncommon for white professors or white supervisors to ask people of color, "What do YOUR people think?" Or, they are only asked of their thoughts when a particular topic related to race is discussed.

Related to this concept of singling out people of color or other people from *disadvantaged* groups, is not directly asking them what they think, but rather to stare at them for their reaction.

In group discussions it is common for someone to say, "I wonder what (fill in the blank) people think of that," and then consciously or unconsciously look at members of that group expecting a response. Although this is less direct than the example in the above paragraph, the impact is the same.

BEST BET

Ask them what they think as an individual rather than as a spokesperson for "their" group. Instead of asking a Jewish person, "What do Jewish people think?" direct the question at the personal level, "What do you think?" or "What has your experience been?" It is important not only to change your words, it is vital that you shift your intent as well. Ultimately if the person feels that your questions are intended for them to be a "spokesperson," the quality of your interaction with them will significantly diminish.

7. "WHAT ARE YOU?" Or "WHERE ARE YOU 'REALLY' FROM?"

INTENTION

We usually have made an assumption based on their accent or how they look, that they are not from the United States, and we are trying to satisfy our curiosity or start a conversation.

IMPACT

These questions are commonly asked of people of Asian descent. When asked where they are from, they may respond by saying the state in which they live only to be asked again, "No, where are you REALLY from?" Often the person is a second or third generation American and is still repeatedly being asked this question.

Chances are this person has been asked this question more than once and is tired of responding to the assumptions inherent in it. The *Pile On Principle* quickly sets in. This statement implies the person is an outsider even though they are not.

BEST BET

First, try not to make assumptions without having all the relevant information. It is not uncommon to ask people where they are from as a conversation starter. However, white people are rarely challenged about their response. Once you have asked the question, accept people's responses. If they choose to add to their response by sharing more information, let them. Don't play detective.

8. "I DON'T SEE COLOR" Or "I'M COLORBLIND."

INTENTION

This statement is similar to the "I don't think of you as…" comment. By eliminating the color difference, we believe that we have leveled the playing field and are being a fair-minded individual.

IMPACT

This is a terribly naïve remark to make because of course we see color. Usually we do not even make such a statement UNTIL we see color. When white people say this to people of color, you can be fairly certain that it will not be received favorably. From the perspective of the person of color, white people are attempting to eliminate race from the conversation. This renders the person of color invisible and dismisses their life experience, which results in mistrust. To deny obvious racial differences is a poignant example of how people from *advantaged* groups, in this instance white people, have the privilege of choosing when, and if, they want to deal with race.

BEST BET

We all know the color we are, so there is no need to pretend we don't. Noticing color is not the problem, but it's rather what we do or say once we notice differences that matters most. There is really no need to state that you are colorblind as it is just not true, no matter how well-intended you might be.

9. "YOU ARE SO ARTICULATE."

INTENTION

This is meant as a compliment or as a testament to someone's verbal skills. People are genuinely surprised when others take offense to this remark.

IMPACT

This comment is usually directed towards people who defy negative stereotypes. If this statement has a negative impact on the person to whom you are speaking, chances are this is not the first time someone has underestimated their capabilities. The person making this comment is surprised to discover that the other person is more intelligent and competent than initially presumed. This is condescending and belittling which results in the person being insulted.

BEST BET

Politicians, especially white men, fall into this well meaning trap when commenting on their opponent's speaking skills. Repeatedly this comment is met with disfavor. Simple statements such as "Great job" or "Nicely done" can convey the message without implying possible racist or sexist overtones which are condescending.

10. "IT IS SO MUCH BETTER THAN IT USED TO BE. JUST BE PATIENT."

INTENTION

The intent behind this statement is to decrease the level of stress and to relax the person who is upset with the obvious inequity they feel about society.

IMPACT

This remark can be condescending and belittling. Such statements paint a picture of the person who is addressing the injustice as a whiner who is never satisfied with all the changes that have already happened. Suggesting they be patient because "We have come so far," will actually increase their frustration. It inherently demands the person who is experiencing the inequity, to be more grateful for changes which have already occurred. Bottom line is you may as well tell the person to shut up and quit their complaining.

BEST BET

Acknowledge the person's comments, but don't try to fix it. Offering sincere statements such as "Some days it must feel like very little progress has been made" or "What can we do to help speed things up now?" will most likely be well received.

The person may feel that you have heard their concerns and a connection will be forged.

11. "YOU SPEAK THE LANGUAGE VERY WELL."

INTENTION

This is used as an acknowledgement of and a compliment to the person who is assumed to be an English language learner.

IMPACT

This statement is a form of racial profiling disguised as a compliment, even if it is not intended that way. It is disturbing because it implies that the person to whom the comment is directed at doesn't look or sound American, and is therefore from another country. It also asserts that there is a proper way to speak English and that all native English speakers are proficient in English.

BEST BET

If English is not the primary language of the person to whom you are making this statement, then this can be taken as a compliment. It becomes a bit more problematic when this statement is directed towards people whose primary language is English; it then is assumed otherwise based on racial assumptions.

As an example, I was in a training workshop and the facilitator was a second generation Japanese American woman who speaks without an accent. She said that many people tell her that she "Speaks the language very well," to which she replies, "I hope so! I've lived here all my life!"

In the United States we have one of the most diverse populations in the world. Be cautious of some of the assumptions being made.

12. ASKING BLACK PEOPLE ABOUT THEIR HAIR OR HYGIENE.

INTENT

This is said out of simple curiosity or to demonstrate interest.

IMPACT

If you are white, this is one sure way to alienate black people, especially black women. Some people even go so far as to touch their hair without permission. Black people are constantly being asked about their hair; "How do you comb it? How often do you wash it? How do you straighten it? How can you have short hair one day and long the next? What are dreadlocks all about?" etc. This is not only an invasion of people's privacy, it also objectifies and dehumanizes them. To reach out without permission can imply disrespect for a person's personal boundaries.

BEST BET

Curiosity is one thing. This is where the role of *allies* can be a great asset. White people asking other white people if they have information regarding these questions serves many positive purposes. First, it lessens the angst white people might have in asking an uncomfortable question. Whites feel far more comfortable asking other white people questions about race because they feel less judged and the fear of offending people of color does not exist.

Second, the fewer times people of color are asked these kinds of questions, the less likely the concept of *P.O.P.* will come into play.

For white people who are unable to find other white people who have this information, there is always the internet. Just Google it!

13. SAYING TO GAY/LESBIAN/BISEXUAL AND TRANSGENDER PEOPLE, "WHAT YOU DO IN THE PRIVACY OF YOUR OWN BEDROOM IS YOUR BUSINESS."

INTENT

People making this statement are usually trying to convey that people's sexual orientation is none of their business and they can live their life as they see fit.

IMPACT

This is an effective way to bring what may be an already uncomfortable conversation to an abrupt halt. Usually this statement is hurtful and annoying. Too often Gay/Lesbian/Bisexual/Transgender (GLBT) people are stereotyped as being overly sexual in nature. When people make the statement, "What you do in the privacy of your own bedroom is your business," there is little acknowledgement of the quality and depth of the relationships which exist outside the confines of the bedroom. Being GLBT is much more that what may or may not happen in the bedroom. To suggest this is hurtful and insulting. Bottom line? You are right; it is not anyone's business, yet you rarely hear that same statement directed towards heterosexuals.

BEST BET

Usually this statement of "What you do in your own bedroom…" is made in response to a conversation or remark about other GLBT issues. It is a better bet to direct your attention and comments towards that topic than to interject this comment. If you are uncomfortable talking about GLBT issues and concerns, simply state that fact instead of making a harmful remark. You can say that you don't have a lot of information and/or experience when it comes to GLBT concerns, and that you don't want to offend someone out of ignorance.

14. "YES, BUT YOU'RE A 'GOOD' ONE."

INTENT

This is the classic "exception to the rule" comment. We think we are offering a compliment, but we are not. We are unconsciously comparing this person to other people within "their group" and find this person to be exceptional and therefore acceptable.

IMPACT

This person may take offense because you are insulting their entire group, and it is clear to them that you find the rest of their group to be bad. Consider this example: imagine saying to a person who is a Muslim, "But you're a good one." It is reasonable for them to conclude that in order for them to be a "good one," the rest of Muslims must be bad ones.

This statement also implies that the reason they are "a good one" is because they are more like you and less like people from their own group. The message here is as long as the other person assimilates and becomes more like your group, the better they are.

BEST BET

Chances are good that if you are making such a statement, you probably do not have a lot of interaction or experiences interacting with the group of people to which this person is a member. Every group of people has "good ones" and "bad ones," and no one group has a disproportionate amount of "bad ones." If you must make a statement, a better point to make is to acknowledge that you know little of the Muslim religion, and if you say anything offensive out of ignorance, ask them to please let you know.

15. "YOU HAVE SUCH A PRETTY FACE."

INTENT

This is usually said to people who are "overweight" as a way to pay them a compliment, and to offer them hope that if they just lose some weight then the rest of their body could be pretty as well.

IMPACT

This statement infers that the person who is "overweight" has so much "potential..." if only they weren't fat. They are not viewed as good enough exactly as they are. We are all taught the code that if you are being set up on a date with someone you have not met, and you ask your friend what the other person looks like, there are two responses that are the kiss of death. One is she/he has a "pretty" or "handsome" face. The other is they have a "great sense of humor." We are taught to read into this statement that the person is overweight and therefore we are looking for other redeemable features or qualities.

BEST BET

Most of us really need to check our assumptions and prejudices around issues of size and physical appearance. Unfortunately, it is still socially acceptable to make derogatory comments on people's size or appearance. No one should be judged on the basis of their color, gender or nationality, and no one should be judged on their physical size or appearance either.

16. "I NEVER OWNED SLAVES."

INTENT

This statement is often used by white people and is usually said out of frustration. Many whites feel they are unjustly accused of being the sole reason racism exists. Two statements often used by white people to convey this sentiment: "I never owned slaves so don't blame this whole mess on me," and "Racism happened long ago so it is time to let it go."

IMPACT

This is a sure fire way to alienate and anger people of color. First, it really is a naive statement, as if there was any doubt that you personally have ever owned a slave. It is safe to say that they realize you do not own slaves. People of color usually see this for what it is, a way for white people to avoid acknowledging that racism still exists today and not to accept their part in perpetuating it.

BEST BET

As a white person, if you are frustrated for being blamed for racism just say that, instead of taking a cheap shot with the slavery comment. In a conversational tone share some of the reasons for your frustrations, while also acknowledging the fact that racism is still alive and well today. You may also start the conversation by saying "These are some of my frustrations and I would be eager to hear some of your frustrations as well."

17. "IF YOU ARE GOING TO LIVE IN THIS COUNTRY, LEARN TO SPEAK THE LANGUAGE!"

INTENT

This speaks to the heart of the immigration issue and the English only movement. This comment creates an "Us vs. Them" mentality. For some people who speak English as their primary language, there is little patience for people who are English language learners and who speak with an accent. They view it as a personal inconvenience to have to work harder to try to understand the other person. Some people believe they are justified to invalidate another person's right to be in this country.

Also, the person making this statement may be resentful that their ancestors may have given up their native language and learned English. If they had to change their language, than so should everyone else.

IMPACT

This comment marginalizes the English language learner. There are also racial undertones which can be in play here. We tend to value or tolerate some accents more than others. For example, we may be less likely to get impatient with someone with a French or British accent than with someone who has a Spanish accent.

BEST BET

There are two issues in play here. The first is people who do not speak English, and the other is people who speak English, but speak with an accent.

Without question, it is always a good idea to learn the primary language of the country in which you are going to live, yet the heart of this statement implies that everyone should speak English. When many Americans travel to countries where English is not the primary language, many get upset because they think everyone, not just Americans, but everyone should speak English. There is a certain indignation towards those who have not mastered the English language.

The irony of this statement is that many people who immigrate into the United States speak more than one language. Despite this, they are still viewed as inferior or ignorant.

We are a country of immigrants. Many of our ancestors did not speak English upon arrival and definitely had an accent at one point. Unfortunately, they were encouraged and at times, forced to forego their native language and speak English only, which is the root of this statement.

18. "SHE/HE IS A GOOD PERSON. SHE/HE DIDN'T MEAN ANYTHING BY IT."

INTENT

This statement serves two purposes. First, it is trying to alleviate the harm that may have been experienced by the person who has been hurt or slighted. Second, it is giving the person who made the comment the benefit of the doubt.

IMPACT

So what if the person is a good person? Good people hurt other people all of the time, yet this does not eradicate the harm they cause. Saying this also has the effect of wiping away the negative comment as not valid and suggests that the person who is offended just needs to let it go. Ultimately it is very dismissive and invalidates the person who is impacted.

BEST BET

Just because someone doesn't mean to hurt you, doesn't mean it still doesn't hurt. The world is full of good people who cause harm, both intentionally and unintentionally. Just acknowledge the harm that has been caused and ask about the impact it has had on the person who was harmed.

19. "WHEN I'VE SAID THE SAME THING TO OTHER PEOPLE LIKE YOU, THEY DIDN'T MIND."

INTENT

When we make a statement like this, it is because we are feeling defensive over a remark we just made that upset someone, and we are attempting to rationalize that it is okay we said it. We are inferring that the problem was not with the comment or joke, but that the person to whom the remark was directed is being over-sensitive.

The person asking this question might also be experiencing genuine confusion as to why it is okay to say something to one person from a certain identity group and how another person from that same group could be offended by the same comment.

IMPACT

This type of statement will usually bring about anger. Not only is the person who made the offensive comment not taking responsibility for it, but they also have the nerve to judge someone for their reaction. This statement seeks to pit members of the same group against one another, which diverts the attention from the person who has caused the disruption to begin with.

BEST BET

Very little good will ever come from making this statement. If someone takes offense to something that you have said, simply apologize. You do not have to make it a bigger deal. You don't even have to make the apology very elaborate, as long as it is sincere.

20. CALLING WOMEN "GIRLS, HONEY, SWEETIE PIE," OR OTHER FAMILIAR TERMS.

INTENT

This statement is usually said by men with the intent to make a connection or attempting to make an environment more casual or friendly.

IMPACT

It is likely that this comment will be perceived as sexist and condescending. There is a feeling of disrespect caused by using terms of endearments inappropriately, especially with colleagues. This statement transcends age differences as well. It is not uncommon for younger men to refer to older women and women who are his subordinates in this fashion. A woman experiences it as paternalistic; as if she is not strong enough or competent enough to take care of herself.

Men often tend to step into a bigger hole when the woman tells him that she does not like being called "honey," "sweetie," etc., and he responds by saying Dumb Thing #19. He tells her that he has made the same statement or called other women "sweetie pie" and they loved it. You have now totally disrespected her and have cranked things up a notch, causing more disruption and discomfort. You have directly or indirectly painted her as a "bitch."

BEST BET

Save terms of endearments for friends and loved ones, not colleagues. Using such familiar terms signifies an element of power. Whether intended or not, it has a way of minimizing the authority of women. I recall watching a program where a male senator referred to a female senator as "sweetie" in his rebuttal to her comments. In this case, his power play was very obvious to most by his attempt to undermine her authority. If she had confronted him in front of millions of viewers on his action of calling her "sweetie," many people may have felt she was being overly sensitive or some sort of feminist who couldn't take a harmless "compliment." If a woman doesn't call him on using these terms, then the man may get away with using the term and undermining some of her power.

21. WHEN PEOPLE OF COLOR SAY, "IT'S NOT THE SAME THING."

INTENT

This statement is commonly made by people of color when Gay, Lesbian, Bisexual, and Transgender (GLBT) people try to liken the experience of racism to heterosexism (discrimination based on sexual orientation). People who are transgender often are discriminated against as a result of people's heterosexism, despite the fact that sexual orientation may not be the issue, but rather gender identity. Some people of color will explain that they did not choose their color and that GLBT people "chose" to be gay, and therefore have to live with the consequences of their choice. Also, it is argued that many GLBT people can "pass" as heterosexual, and do not have to let people know their sexual orientation, but they, as a person of color, can never pass as anything but what they are and will be judged everyday on their race.

IMPACT

This is disheartening, not only to the GLBT community, but especially to the people of color in the GLBT community. Audre Lorde, a black lesbian author and activist, talks about there not being any hierarchy of oppression. Yet people from different oppressed groups continue to struggle with one another as to whose oppression is worse. Many GLBT people are fully aware that the dynamics of race and orientation discrimination are different. However, the impact is the same.

It stands to reason that if you are from a group who has been historically oppressed, you would have more compassion and share camaraderie with others from different oppressed groups. Sadly, however, this is often not the case. When people of color who are also heterosexual make such a statement, it is clear that they are distancing themselves from their own homophobia and not taking responsibility for it. They do not understand the huge discrepancy and contradiction they are making by fighting racism while contributing to the oppression of another group. People of color often grow impatient and angry at white people for not accepting their own racism or for doing some self-education. By saying, "But this is not the same issue" to the GLBT community, keeps us from building coalitions between different groups so that we can forge alliances and form critical masses for change.

BEST BET

Just as people of color want white people to work on their own racism and fight for social justice, people who are GLBT expect the same from their heterosexual counterparts. As we all work on our heterosexism, we are then able to move on to the larger vision of social justice for all. Reverend Dr. Martin Luther King Jr. stated it well when he said that "Injustice anywhere is a threat to justice everywhere."

22. WHEN PEOPLE OF FAITH SAY, "LOVE THE SINNER, HATE THE SIN."

INTENT

This can be said as an attempt to reach out in a compassionate way to GLBT (Gay, Lesbian, Bisexual and Transgender) people while not condoning their action or their "choice."

IMPACT

First, it must be stated that being GLBT and a person of faith are not mutually exclusive. This fact can be troubling to people on both sides of this discussion. For instance, many religious people cannot or will not understand how "homosexuals" can in good conscience be a member of a religious organization, while doing things that religious people feel are morally wrong and against their religious teachings.

On the other side, people who are GLBT and belong to faith based organizations, may battle against many non-religious GLBT people who question how they can be a part of a religious organization that mistreats them and calls them sinners. Either way, GLBT people of faith face challenges from both sides of the aisle.

That being said, for many GLBT people it is very difficult to make sense of the contradiction that religious people are not supposed to judge others and do no harm - tenants that are common to most religions. As a result, people of faith are often viewed as hypocrites, because their words and their deeds are inconsistent.

BEST BET

Sometimes the best we can do is to agree to disagree. Recognizing that organized religion has been used historically to support not only heterosexism, but also racism, sexism and anti-Semitism, can forge the way for meaningful dialogue. It is best to leave the judging for judgment day, if indeed you believe in such a day.

23. WHEN WHITE MEN SAY, "WE ARE THE ONES WHO ARE BEING DISCRIMINATED AGAINST NOW!"

INTENT

Typically people who make this sort of statement are frustrated by the lack of acknowledgement that discrimination has an impact on all people, not just those from underrepresented groups. And more to the point, that white men in particular are serving as scapegoats for all of society's ills.

IMPACT

This statement will quickly stir the pot for most people with *disadvantaged* identities. It can be likened to the actions of the spoiled child who doesn't always get what they want so they whine. For people from disadvantaged identities, it is tempting to say to white men, "How does it feel to be on the other end of the stick?"

There is a difference between discrimination and oppression. A major distinction is that all people can be discriminated against at a personal level. However, when it comes to institutional power and cultural norms, it is the people who make the rules who benefit from the rules. Bottom line is that white men still experience more privileges than any other group. You only have to look at our government and corporate structures to get a clear sense of entitlement.

BEST BET

White men should use this experience to gain insight as to how it feels to be marginalized. This demonstration of empathy and understanding will forge relationships that are built on trust and mutual respect. Truth be told, if you want people to understand your experience and feelings, it is sometimes best to understand their own first, as then they are more likely to listen and be open to hearing your experience.

Also, it is important to acknowledge how privilege benefits you. This can be especially challenging for white men who are from other disadvantaged groups, as they are tempted to talk about that experience and avoid discussions on their privilege as a white man. Remember, privilege is not something we always have control of; it is given not earned. By acknowledging your privilege, you demonstrate your awareness of a system of inequity.

24. REFERRING TO OLDER PEOPLE AS "CUTE."

INTENT

Referring to older people as "cute" is meant as a compliment and a form of flattery.

IMPACT

Both the tone and the use of this word are condescending. We sometimes talk to older people the same way we talk to little children. This belittles them and at times can be very humiliating to the older person.

BEST BET

Respect is a concept which transcends age. At times we forget that even though a person's body has aged, inside that body is someone who has had a lifetime of experience and knowledge that can benefit anyone with whom they come in contact. Perhaps there is a good deal of truth in the saying, "With age comes wisdom." Take advantage of the opportunity to connect with this person as it will be a "win-win" situation for both of you.

25. ASKING A TRANSGENDER PERSON, "WHAT ARE YOU REALLY? ARE YOU A MAN OR A WOMAN?"

INTENT

There is usually genuine confusion by the person asking this question. They are seeking clarification of the person's gender so they can identify how to treat that person appropriately.

IMPACT

People who do not visibly conform to gender roles and expectations are challenged and harassed daily. This question only compounds the invisibility that many transgender people face on a daily basis. Adding "really" to this question of gender implies that the transgender person may be deceiving you intentionally.

Note that in terms of impact, not all transgender people face invisibility. Rather it is their visibility that is the problem. There is a price to pay for being visibly "different," (i.e. not being able to easily use public rest room facilities that are designated for men/ women; being judged in every social interaction, etc).

BEST BET

For most people, gender identity and gender expression are seen as a very dualistic concept: you are either male or you are female, or a man or a woman - case closed. However, this issue is much more fluid and encompasses a wide range of experiences. These experiences include, but are not limited to, people who identify as being transgender, transsexual, gender non-conforming, gender queer, cross-dressing, butch and femme. Instead of asking the above questions, ask what pronouns the person prefers, and then use those pronouns and encourage others to do so.

26. REFERRING TO THE SIGNIFICANT OTHER, PARTNER OR SPOUSE, OF A SAME GENDER COUPLE AS THEIR "FRIEND."

INTENT

At times, using the term "friend" is the result of not knowing the vocabulary of the preferred term for same gender couples. Also, it might be a way of not making assumptions as to the nature of the relationship if it is unclear to the person addressing them.

IMPACT

Using "friend" minimizes the depth of the relationship. It leaves the GLBT person feeling marginalized and disrespected. Most likely you would not refer to a heterosexual's spouse as "their friend."

BEST BET

With the exception of the state of Massachusetts, same gender couples cannot have their marriages legally validated in the United States. The language use of "Mr. and Mrs." which we have grown accustomed to using in heterosexual marriages, simply does not apply. It is best to ask the person how they refer to that person. As their partner? Significant other? Husband? Wife? Spouse? Most same gender couples have gone through the process of choosing the language that best describes their relationship and as a result may be open to you asking what language is preferred. Let them define their own language and not have you assign it to them.

27. "WHY DO 'THEY' (FILL IN THE BLANK) ALWAYS HAVE TO SIT TOGETHER? THEY ARE ALWAYS STICKING TOGETHER."

INTENT

At some level we might feel excluded and wonder why "they" never sit with us. It can feel as though "they" are part of some exclusive little group or club that we have not been invited to.

IMPACT

It is important to define who "they" are when this statement is used. The "they" in this case is often used by people in the majority and directed towards people in the minority. People who are in the majority are rarely accused of clumping. In fact, one of the privileges of being in the majority is that you don't have to think about a statement like this being directed towards you. Even more challenging is that this comment is usually given in an accusatory tone and carries a good deal of judgment.

Even if we do not come right out and ask "them" why they always sit together, we tend to give other signals such as our non-verbal behavior, staring and hushed tones that indicate we disapprove of them. This can lead to feelings of resentment and inequity and suggests there is a double standard of social norms. When people in the majority are together, they are seen as "just hanging out together" - there are no judgments made. However, when people who are in the minority are together, it as though the majority feels that the other group is plotting against them somehow.

BEST BET

ALL people "clump" - it is part of the human condition. We clump with people whom we have something in common. Sometimes you can visually see the commonality as in race or gender, and other times the reason may be less obvious such as religion, ability, sexual orientation, socio-economic class or even things like political affiliations or civic organizations. Clumping is not the problem; in fact it is natural. The problem is when we begin to pass judgment as to who is allowed to clump together.

This notion of clumping is expanded on in the closing chapter, Smart Steps For Well-Intended People, Step #5 - We are all "multi-clumpable."

28. "PEOPLE JUST NEED TO PICK THEMSELVES UP BY THEIR BOOTSTRAPS."

INTENT

People making this comment are suggesting that if people do not like their lot in life, then they need to work harder to change it.

IMPACT

This statement lacks an acknowledgement of the reality that some people have been given an advantage simply by their social identity, and that some people have to work twice as hard to achieve the same level of success. For example, there are many people who are hourly wage earners and work sixty hours a week yet still have a hard time keeping their head above water.

BEST BET

Many of us make the assumption that people who are poor or of moderate means are simply lazy and therefore deserve what they get. We equate how hard we work with how much money we make. Reality tells us that there is a huge disparity between jobs that have value and those that do not. One only needs to look at how much professional athletes and movie stars are paid compared to working class and middle class people to begin to understand the disparity. It is evident to many that we need to move away from a "minimum wage" to a "living wage."

29. PEOPLE WITH DISABILITIES ARE "COURAGEOUS."

INTENT

This is meant as a sincere compliment and acknowledgement of the barriers that some people experience in society.

IMPACT

This statement paints the person with the disability as superhuman, and can be experienced as condescending. Imagine saying to a woman, "You are courageous" simply for the fact that she is a woman. Even though there are barriers which women face due to sexism, the reality is she gets up every morning and lives her life. The same is true for people with disabilities.

BEST BET

For people with disabilities, maneuvering through a world which is not accommodating and easily accessible is a daily occurrence. These barriers take different forms with regards to accessibility and attitudes. Accessibility issues include, but are not limited to, physical barriers with regard to mobility. We commonly associate people who are wheelchair users or people who have difficulty in walking with these physical barriers. Yet accessibility concerns are far more reaching than the one dimensional notion which able-bodied people have. People who experience visual or hearing impairments or people with developmental disabilities, have a host of different barriers than those who cannot walk.

For instance, in order for a residence to be accessible for people with mobility concerns, improvements to the dwelling may include things like an accessible shower. Such a shower does not involve the person having to step up and includes a seat. Counters and cabinets are also built lower to accommodate someone sitting in a chair.

For a person who is hearing impaired, accessibility would include having a fire alarm that not only emits sound, but also blinks intensely.

Beyond physical barriers, people with disabilities also experience limitations from able-bodied people's attitudes. Attitudinal barriers are equally limiting.

Many of us are taught that when we see someone who has an obvious disability we are not to stare. In theory, this is good advice as no one likes to be stared at, and people with disabilities are no different. However, people without disabilities are so afraid of staring that they translate "Don't stare" into "Don't look." As a result, it is not uncommon for people to defer their eye contact, look away quickly, or even pull their children away from people with disabilities in order to be polite. This constant neglect results in invisibility. What started out as a well-intended act of kindness results in an unintended, but misguided, act of cruelty.

There are many people who have inspired us with the ways they have dealt with adversity and have overcome the odds. It is important to honor that person and their story. It is when we build caricatures of people and paint the stereotype with a broad stroke from the same paintbrush that it diminishes the actual person.

30. "THAT'S SO GAY/QUEER" Or "THAT'S SO RETARDED."

INTENT

More and more these statements are viewed as common expressions and people making these statements don't mean any harm.

IMPACT

Both of these statements and others like them are derogatory by nature. They are meant to demean the person they are directed towards and result in hurting so many more who also hear the comment. Whether or not someone within earshot is gay, or has a developmental disability is not important.

Many statements like these have found their way into our daily language. There is no recognition that they are hurtful, nor is there an acknowledgment to their historically negative connotation.

Those who make these statements usually are defensive when confronted about their offensive comments. Usually they say they didn't mean anything by it. This creates *P.O.P.* as described in the 10 Core Concepts. A bad situation is made worse because you have not accepted responsibility for causing harm.

BEST BET

There is a familiar saying, "Sticks and stones may break my bones, but names will never hurt me." I wish that were true, but for so many of us, we can recall when we were kids some of the names and words aimed at us which caused a good deal of personal harm. A more accurate saying might be, "Sticks and stones may break my bones, but words can scar a lifetime." Words are always evolving, but there are many words that despite their common usage are still just hurtful.

Choosing descriptions which do not ridicule people is easy. Perhaps saying things like, "That's odd" or "You're acting like a knucklehead" is far less offensive.

31. "I DON'T SEE DIFFERENCE. WE'RE ALL PART OF THE SAME RACE, THE HUMAN RACE."

INTENT

This is another statement reinforcing the idea that the person making this comment treats all people the same and does not discriminate.

IMPACT

People of color can experience this statement as another way for white people to render them invisible. As a result, many people of color will have very little patience and tolerance for such a remark.

Making a comment such as this dismisses and denies the reality of race, privilege and discrimination. It is an easy way for white people to avoid the conversation of race and privilege. After all, if you do not acknowledge that a problem exists then you don't have to do anything to fix it!

BEST BET

Let's break down this commonly used statement. The first part, "I don't see difference", is very similar to Dumb Things #8, "I don't see color, I am colorblind." It has a tendency to eliminate or minimize racial differences. The second part of this statement, "We're all part of the same race, the human race," proposes the person making this statement envisions an ideal world - a world where race is seen as just another dimension of a person's identity and experience.

However, we currently do not live in such a world. We need to acknowledge that even though we are all part of the "same race, the human race," we are not all treated with the same level of dignity and respect.

Acknowledging a person's racial identity is natural; there is no need to minimize their experience. Race is a significant part of a person's identity and experience. It informs others about how we see and experience the world.

32. "I DON'T CARE IF YOU ARE PINK, PURPLE OR ORANGE, I TREAT ALL PEOPLE THE SAME."

INTENT

So many of the "Dumb Things" we say are an effort to let people know that we are not bigots and that we do not discriminate on the basis of "whatever." We want the person to know that things like race, gender, age, religion, etc. are not relevant.

IMPACT

Even if we believe that race, gender, age, religion, etc., do not influence how we treat people, the reality is they do impact our experience. Some people might suggest that it doesn't matter if someone is poor; that everyone is treated with the same level of respect as rich people. It is worth noting that it is usually the rich person who is offering this perspective.

This statement totally dismisses the person's differences as insignificant, which results in anger and frustration. Since there are no "pink, purple or orange" people in the world, it's probably wise to stay away from such an analogy.

BEST BET

Go about your business in a way that acknowledges and respects our differences as well as our commonalities. As a result, you will not have to make such statements that risk minimizing people's experience. At times, people need you to embrace their differences as well as their commonalities.

33. ASKING A TRANSGENDER PERSON, "HAVE YOU HAD THE OPERATION?"

INTENT

This statement seeks clarification of a person's gender and erroneously implies that in order to be transgender, one must have had "the" operation.

IMPACT

It is important to recognize that you are asking a very personal question. Asking questions about surgery are inappropriate unless you have a very close relationship with the person you're addressing. By asking "What are you really?" or "What is your real name?" you're assuming that you are entitled to an explanation from the person. This may add to the harassment and tension of their everyday life experience. Such harassment has often led to violence.

BEST BET

Transgender people are not lying or attempting to deceive; they are living their lives true to themselves. It is extremely difficult and expensive to access medical or social interventions. To be an ally to transgender people, we must support the many ways people can express gender. Ask what pronouns the person prefers and use their choice which may differ from their given name. Promote the use of unisex or gender neutral bathrooms. Offer support when there are difficulties with family members or others around you in accepting the transgender person.

34. SAYING TO A JEWISH PERSON, "YOU ARE SO LUCKY TO HAVE 'YOUR' CHRISTMAS SPREAD OVER A WEEK!"

INTENT

The person making this statement is acknowledging that Chanukah is a holiday observed by people who are Jewish and is celebrated around the same time as Christmas. The person may be genuinely inquiring about the traditions in an effort to demonstrate an appreciation and awareness of Chanukah.

IMPACT

Unfortunately this shows a clear lack of understanding about Chanukah which is not the Jewish equivalent to Christmas. Chanukah is a minor holiday in the Jewish religion when compared to Rosh Hashanah, Yom Kippur and Passover. Chanukah has gained importance in the United States simply because it falls so close to Christmas. The linking of Chanukah and Christmas can be frustrating and upsetting to Jews. There is no recognition that the holidays which are important to them do not receive the same societal and cultural support as Christian holidays. Societal and cultural support is given to the Christmas holidays through such things as time off from work and school to celebrate with family without having to take a vacation or personal day, Christmas music, decorations, parties, etc.

BEST BET

If you are unsure about the traditional or religious holidays people celebrate ask, "Do you and/or your family celebrate the holidays? If so, how?" If you know for certain that they celebrate Chanukah, offer them a Happy Chanukah!

35. "HERE IS ANOTHER BOOK ON 'POLITICAL CORRECTNESS'."

INTENT

Some people are frustrated with being told what they can and cannot say, and as a result try to diminish the value of the information being offered.

IMPACT

Labeling something as "politically correct" is a common and powerful way to dismiss an experience or viewpoint. The person making the comment about political correctness is attempting to shut the other person up so that they "shut down" and they no longer have to deal with them. It demonstrates impatience and unwillingness to learn new ways to have more effective communication.

The most significant impact of this thinking is that it continues to widen the divide of "us versus them." We tend to shut down our minds and our hearts to hearing and understanding other people's perspectives that are different from our own.

BEST BET

Einstein said that "We are all ignorant, just in different areas." We are all lifelong learners and teachers. The more we learn, the better we can teach compassion to the next generation.

"You can put up the sail, but if the anchor is still down you are not going to get very far!"

MAURA J CULLEN

SIX SMART STEPS FOR WELL-INTENDED PEOPLE

Chapter Four

We have explored some of the core concepts as a way to understand why people sometimes get offended by the "Dumb Things" we say. Now we will finish by looking at strategies to assist you in your successful interactions with others.

It is my hope that you have come to understand that all of us at some point in our lives have made many of the statements described in this book. It is not so much that they are "dumb" things to say, but rather they are things we say out of ignorance. Now that you have been given more information and a better

113

understanding of just how much of an impact these statements can have on people, you must decide what to do next.

With this intention in mind, I offer these 6 simple strategies for taking some of the adversity out of diversity dialogues.

1. START WITH THE END IN MIND

When we are trying to find our way to any destination we always start with the end in mind. Once you have made the decision of where you want to end up, the process of getting there becomes much clearer. For instance, if I am in New York and I want to get to Boston, I would look at a map (or these days a GPS), and decide on a route. It may be a direct route or one that takes a bit more time, but is more enjoyable. Either way, I will arrive in Boston.

Discussions around diversity are much the same. Once you have decided what you would like the outcome to look like, then you can work backwards and decide which route you will take. Sometimes we do not have the luxury of taking the leisurely route, which would certainly be more enjoyable, but may not be the most effective. There will be times when someone says a very inappropriate comment, or acts in an inappropriate manner and immediate action is deemed necessary. This direct approach can be uncomfortable for many to enforce. Doing the right thing is not always the easiest or popular path to walk. In fact, people often find themselves alone on this road less traveled, as it takes a good deal of personal fortitude to stay on it and keep moving forward.

Other days, we have the luxury of taking our time in being more deliberate with our diversity interventions. There is no immediate "crisis" occurring, so we can be more proactive in our educational efforts towards building a more inclusive environment. It is during these times when our efforts should be focused on planning policies and training efforts. Long term strategies for success have a much higher probability of succeeding during non-crisis times than that of crisis management.

Like many things in life, the more we do something, the easier it becomes and the better we become at doing it. The more we intervene when witnessing injustice or unkind acts, the more skilled we become and the easier it gets. But the process of gaining these skills and becoming more culturally competent can take some time and we will make mistakes along the way.

One of the more successful techniques I have used to strengthen my ability and willingness to confront acts of intolerance is to reframe a successful intervention. For too long, I would become disappointed because my attempts to change the other person's viewpoint or actions were not going as I had planned. From my perspective, if the person did not immediately change and rectify their position, then I had failed. Needless to say, I failed a lot.

In order to continue my work as an *ally*, I had to reframe the definition of a successful intervention. I now realize that the actual intervention is more important than the outcome. As long as I do or say something to acknowledge the harm, then I have been successful. A critical lesson for me to learn was that I haven't any control over how people respond to me. The only thing I have control over is how I respond to other people.

By starting with the end in mind, we have a clearer understanding of the direction we want the conversation to take. This will guide the decisions and choices we make along the way as we move towards our ultimate destination of compassion and integrity.

2. SHIFT YOUR THINKING FROM "ME" TO "WE"

When someone says or does something that evokes a strong reaction in us, it is natural to give an immediate response. This response has us focusing on ourselves instead of seeking clarification from the other person. As soon as we become self-absorbed, we are diminishing the odds of making a connection with the other person to whom we are trying to build a rapport.

*"To build inclusive organizations
there must be a shift from "me" to "we"."*

MAURA J CULLEN

Instead of making the focus of the conversation about "me," try moving it to the "we" level.

For example, sometimes a man will refer to a woman as a "girl." Although not intended, this leaves some women feeling dismissed and not respected. As a result the woman may respond in one of three ways. First, she may choose to ignore the comment even though it bothered her. If it is the first time this particular man may have said it to her, she is likely to cut him some slack, but still carry that memory into future experiences with him. Second, she could become very assertive and confrontational. After all, it is most likely not the first time she has had the experience of a man demonstrating his dominance in this manner.

Lastly, she could verbally respond to the man, letting him know that referring to her as a "girl" is belittling, and that it would be similar to people in power repeatedly referring to him as a "boy." Using the word "boy" and "girl" when referring to actual children is fine. However, when speaking of adults, using these terms can be disrespectful.

By choosing the last option, the interaction is successful on a number of levels. First, the woman gets to speak her mind and let the man know the comment was not appreciated. Second, the man may not have realized using "girl" is offensive to some women and now he is armed with useful information in order to make different choices in the future. Third, by taking it from the "me" perspective and transferring into the "we" perspective, the woman offered an example that would resonate with the man. Being referred to by people in power as a "boy" may clearly show the man how this term can be offensive.

Conversely, the man can take this same example from the "me" to "we" level by not getting defensive and making it all about him. Often when people have critical feedback for us, we want to offer *explain aways*, or we just get angry. Doing this, however, takes the focus off of the woman in this case, and places it on him. This may cause the woman further upset because the man is not accepting responsibility for the fact that his words caused her harm. Instead, he might be better served by apologizing and seeking further clarification from her about the offensive nature of his words. If she does offer a clarification, then the most important thing the man can do is to LISTEN.

It is unfortunate that people who experience discrimination are frequently put in positions of educator. This simply replicates oppressive dynamics. This discrimination and oppression can be compounded if the man is her supervisor. Power dynamics play an important role in the process of choosing how or if to intervene. However, by practicing this method of direct confrontation, you will experience enormous and immediate results in building stronger connections.

"Integrity is something you must give away,
no one can take it from you."

MAURA J CULLEN

3. NAME IT – CLAIM IT – ACT ON IT

When people are mistreated, one of the first things they look for is an acknowledgement of the offense. An acknowledgement or naming of the offense opens the possibility of dialogue. One of the biggest mistakes people make is to ignore what happened or pretend it didn't happen in hopes that it will just be forgotten. By not naming the offense, the person who is being harmed will think that either you are not insightful enough to understand or that you do not care. Both of these will create mistrust and you are unlikely to forge a significant relationship.

When you screw up, say you screwed up and apologize. Don't try to explain it, negate it, or forget it. Simply name it, claim responsibility and act on it. By doing this you are in a better position of asking what would be helpful or beneficial in righting the wrong. It is impossible to know everything there is to know, so there is no need to pretend otherwise. The most challenging part of this process is being able to let it go once you have apologized. Too many of us hold onto the mistake, which prevents us from moving forward and freeing us up to continue to take risks and learn. By not letting go of your mistake, you can stay stuck in guilt and continue to be a non-productive ally. Once you have named the problem and claimed some responsibility, you are better able to find the next logical step towards creating a relationship built on trust.

Noticing difference is not the problem.

It's what we do once we notice that matters most."

MAURA J CULLEN

4. WE ARE ALL DIFFERENT—
WE ARE ALL THE SAME

The concept of multiple truths is a common yet complicated notion. How can two seemingly competing ideas both be true at the same time? Most would agree that we all have the propensity to be good and bad. Many of us have been in relationships when we clearly liked the person most of the time yet in other moments we couldn't stand them. Two competing or opposite emotions and/or experiences can co-exist together.

When it comes to diversity, one multiple truth is that we are all different and we are all the same. We all have elements or common experiences which we share and others that make us unique or different. Conversations are often started by focusing on either what we have in common or what differs. We need to be mindful of deciding the approach that will work best in creating a connection with the other person.

In social justice and diversity education, some believe that in order to make progress we need to focus on difference or uniqueness.

Others tend to focus their efforts on examining those elements that we have in common. Their thinking is that we need to create a common foundation of shared experiences before moving on to harder discussions.

I have found that the most effective strategy is not to focus solely on one at the exclusion of the other. Instead of creating an "either/or" dichotomy, we must advance to a "both/and" approach. As long as you acknowledge only one of these approaches, you will never be successful in building the bridge essential to connecting the gap between the have's and have not's.

5. WE ARE ALL "MULTI-CLUMPABLE"

When people share something in common, they tend to gather together as a group or as a "clump." We all do it; it is natural. However, sometimes people question why certain groups appear to always be clumping and never "mingle" with others. What many of us fail to recognize is that we also clump most of the time, but because we may be in the majority, we do not perceive it as clumping. In her book, "Why Are All The Black Kids Sitting Together In The Cafeteria?" Dr. Beverly Tatum illustrates just how powerful this notion of clumping can be. Whether at work or school, most of us have asked or thought of a similar question to Tatum's. A less common question is to notice the other 90% of the people in the cafeteria and ask "Why are all the white kids sitting together in the cafeteria?" By not considering the entire context we keep the dynamic of "Us" and "Them" alive and well.

"Valuing diversity starts off as something that we do and grows into something that we are."

Maura J Cullen

It is not unusual to see international students or international colleagues clumping. It makes sense this would occur since they have the shared experience of not being from the United States. What is fascinating is in many instances international people do not share a common language and yet they come together as a community with their differences.

Truth be told, we are all members of many different "clumps" in our lives. Some of these clumps may be related to our social identity such as gender or race. Others are because of our personal beliefs or affiliations such as religion, political and civic organizations, sports or hobbies. Regardless, what we need to understand is that we are all "multi-clumpable" - that we are members of countless groups. If we base our judgments on only one piece of information, we are effectively diminishing the likelihood that we will make a significant connection with other people.

6. HAVE AND MAINTAIN A SENSE OF HUMOR

Having a sense of humor does not imply that we should joke about these very important discussions. There is an important distinction between using humor as a way to forge relationships, and humor that widens the divide and offends people. When

"At times we have to reach around the words

to discover the true intent."

MAURA J CULLEN

used appropriately, humor can forge a relationship and build a strong bond and connection between two people. When used inappropriately, the results can create mistrust. It is the difference between laughing with someone or at someone.

However, sometimes we take ourselves so seriously that we lose sight of what life is all about, that of building connections with others. At times, laughter is just the thing we need to build the bridge.

"Passion + Compassion +Action -
Essential components for long term change."

Maura J Cullen

Conclusion

There comes a time when well-intended people can no longer use the excuse that they didn't know or understand the power of their words and the impact they have on others. The information offered in this book will supply you with a strong base of knowledge and skills so that you can take effective action in building more inclusive organizations and better personal relationships.

As stated in the introduction, often we make things harder than they need to be. If you are the person who always seems to be doing the educating, I know firsthand that it can be extremely frustrating and exhausting. It gets old and tiring to have to serve as the spokesperson for "your" people. At times we simply want to yell "Shut Up!" and be left to ourselves.

Instead we would be well served if we start with the end in mind and understand that even well-intended people cause harm, take a deep breath and employ the power of **B.A.R.** (Breathe, Acknowledge, Respond). At times we have to reach around the words people use to better understand their intent. If the person really didn't mean any harm, then they need to be educated in the most compassionate and respectful way possible. Yet if you do not have the time, energy or inclination to be the "tutor," then it is best to figure a way that can take care of your needs while not causing harm to the person who lacks information. In the end, this is the way most of us would like to be treated when we make mistakes.

Are you the person who seems to be always messing up? I know firsthand that it is extremely frustrating and humiliating to make mistakes. I say I know about these feelings as I've been there – done that, and have learned how to do things differently. We must always remember that well-intended people can cause harm, and when we say something offensive or hurtful, we must acknowledge it. We need to "name it, claim it, and act on it." By "naming it," we acknowledge the offensive statement. After we name it, we need to "claim it" and accept responsibility for our mistake. Then we need to "act on it" to preserve a meaningful interaction. When all is said and done, what we all seek is to be respected and listened to.

When we start with the end in mind, it is much easier to give people the benefit of the doubt. After all, we are looking to build stronger relationships, better organizations and united communities. Most days, people truly are well-intended and doing the best they can. Sadly, sometimes our best is not good enough. Fortunately by enacting some of the changes offered in this book, we have the opportunity to make an immediate and positive impact on those around us everyday.

"Diversity is about creating magic – finding those who have disappeared and helping them re-appear."

MAURA J CULLEN

Closing Thoughts

Do good intentions count for something? Yes. I believe that well-intended statements do count at some level. However, intentions in and of themselves do not eradicate the harmful impact such statements cause. All of us at some point have made well-intentioned statements which have caused harm; it is part of the human experience. Personally, I would much rather deal with someone who has good intentions, than with someone who is purposely doing harm. It is however, not an excuse and should not be used as such.

The list that I've made in this book includes some of the most common statements that act as pitfalls to effective communication. It is my most sincere hope that the information shared has provided you with beneficial insights that will improve the overall quality of your relationships, both personally and professionally. I maintain a strong personal belief that people are basically good hearted and look to help people, not hurt them. Once we realize that we have caused harm, we look to heal it. I leave you with one final quote.

"When other people make mistakes, we seek justice.

When we make mistakes, we seek compassion.

The lesson is to give to others what you seek."

Maura J Cullen

The Next Step...

1. To book Maura for your organizations next event and experience her dynamic keynotes and seminars that transform our diversity conversations, visit www.MauraCullen.com or call 877.230.9318.

2. Invest in your groups or organization's continuing diversity education and receive discounts on bulk purchases of *35 Dumb Things Well-Intended People Say*, email us at Info@MauraCullen.com

3. Go to www.MauraCullen.com to receive the following gifts:
   - Download audio interviews #1 and #2 of the series, "Diversity Mentors"

- Sign up for our free e-newsletter
- Receive your complimentary report, "Seven Steps to Success in Diversity Training"

4. 35 Dumb Things is also available in audio format.

For Availability and Information Contact
Maura Cullen & Associates, LLC, www.MauraCullen.com,
email us at Info@MauraCullen.com
Call us at 877. 230. 9318

About the Author

Maura Cullen is a highly-acclaimed diversity trainer who has educated and inspired people worldwide in over 400 organizations on how to be more inclusive, understanding and authentic when communicating with others. She has over 20 years of experience as a keynote speaker and received her doctorate in Social Justice and Diversity Education from the University of Massachusetts. She has mastered the art of making diversity a simple, tangible, and enjoyable issue for audiences across the country. When not at home in Massachusetts, you will most likely find Maura in the Green Mountain state of Vermont, hiking or snowshoeing with her family and two dogs. Visit Maura online at www.MauraCullen.com.

Printed in
HEAD TEXT

Printed in the United States
140725LV00001B/56/P

9 781600 374913